And Everyone Shall

Praise

And Everyone Shall
Praise

Resources for
Multicultural Worship

R. Mark Liebenow

United Church Press

Cleveland, Ohio

United Church Press, Cleveland, Ohio 44115
© 1999 by R. Mark Liebenow

The bread meditation and music in "Communion Service: A Reflection on This Communion" are used by permission of Kay Ward.

Biblical quotations are from the New Revised Standard Version of the Bible, © 1989 by the Division of Christian Education of the National Council of the Churches of Christ in the U.S.A., and are used by permission. Adapted for inclusivity.

Printed in the United States of America on acid-free paper

04 03 02 01 00 99   5 4 3 2 1

Library of Congress Cataloging-in-Publication Data
Liebenow, R. Mark (Ronald Mark), 1953–
    And everyone shall praise : resources for multicultural worship /
R. Mark Liebenow.
      p.   cm.
   ISBN 0-8298-1318-7 (pbk. : alk. paper)
    1. Worship programs.   2. Multiculturalism—Religious aspects—
Christianity.   I. Title.
   BV198.L47   1999
   264—dc21   99-18722
                                                             CIP

Contents

Preface

All Christian churches observe some part of the church year calendar, if only Christmas and Easter. Many denominations also hold special observances for Advent, Lent, and the day of Pentecost. Some traditions go even further, working out a weekly schedule of church observances throughout the year which incorporates various theological, biblical, historical, and cultural events.

This book offers inclusive and multicultural liturgies, responsive readings, and prayers for the major church observances as well as for many special ones. The tone varies from piece to piece. Some liturgies are formal, some are celebratory, some are meditative. Since no printed liturgy will ever address everything that could be said about something like the day of Pentecost, images and words can be substituted to tailor the material in this book to the needs of your congregation. Even the forms are interchangeable. There are litanies that can be prayed and prayers that can be lined out as responsive readings.

Part One offers practical suggestions and guidelines for worship committees that plan worship services and want to write their own material. It also discusses the use of language in worship. Part Two presents worship resources for the liturgical seasons of the year, highlighting the dynamics of cultural celebrations. The appendix offers a detailed calendar of events for every day of the year.

It's important that we be intentional about the language we use in worship, that we choose a few specific words instead of many general ones to get our message across. It's important that we are creative in our use of metaphors, images, and poetry in our effort to fully worship so that we may come to have "aha" experiences of insight.

May your worship be alive with streams of celebration, struggle, and spirituality that are as nourishing as rivers and as deep as the oceans.

Acknowledgments

The liturgies in this book have been written over a period of years—at first, with no thought to their being published. I have been inspired by many sources. Every effort has been made to acknowledge borrowed material. My thanks to Kay Ward for her permission to use her words and music for "A Reflection on This Communion" liturgy.

My gratitude goes to the Moravian Church, which instilled in me the love of liturgies, to Jack Hicks who helped me see that worship could be creative, and to the multicultural Lakeshore Avenue congregation in Oakland, California, which challenged me to write liturgies and prayers for people of all races and cultures.

Part One

Worship in the Church

Worship Planning

When members of a congregation come together to plan worship, the challenge they face is to create a service that is interesting to all the members of the congregation most of the time, that doesn't offend anyone, and that engages each member's heart, mind, and soul. Meeting this challenge, of course, requires careful planning.

The Worship Committee

The worship committee is responsible for assembling the parts of the worship service in such a way that they flow smoothly from one to another, creating and deepening a sense of worship, involving the congregation in worship planning and presentation, using language responsibly, and presenting services that are not predictable.

A major challenge is to build upon the long tradition of Christian worship without being limited to materials from the past. For example, the old hymns and traditions bring pleasure to those who grew up with them, but they may mean nothing special to new members and may even seem boring or hard to understand. If new material isn't constantly brought into worship, congregations get comfortable worshiping in a set way, with specific patterns and words. Yet within the old hymns and traditions are kernels of faith and spirit that transcend their forms. One goal is to save this material either by using the old music form with new words or putting the old words into new music forms.

There is great value in having members of the committee pull material together for Sunday worship. Sharing worship resources with other churches is another way of gathering ideas. Involving more people in planning worship allows them to use their skills and bring their insights and learning into the worship experience. It also lifts the burden of forced creativity off of the pastor. As a result, the language of faith is enriched with new images and nuances. One of my dreams is for a group of people to come together every Saturday and create the liturgics for Sunday (call to worship, responsive reading, litany, community prayer) by using what has happened in the life of the congregation that week. The result would be a service that not only is timely but which also bridges the gap between daily life and Sunday worship.

There are a few concerns to address with regard to language. What guidelines will you observe in using language? Will you use inclusive language for everything? How politically correct will you be? What concerns will you address in worship, and which ones will you purposely exclude or downplay? For some people, faith is rooted in social action; for others, it is in Bible study. Prayer is the focus for some, while it is community for others. Still others explore their understanding of God through art or nature. The challenge is to blend all these resources of inspiration together so that the social action people draw guidance from the Bible study people, the Bible study people find insights from those creating art, and so on. In this way, everyone learns to value and respect what is important to others, each person has a chance to incorporate something new into his or her walk of faith, and the community is strengthened by the interaction of images. We are members of one body, and we need what others have to offer. Only together do we come close to seeing the fullness of God.

Goals and Expectations of the Worship Committee

The worship committee should meet at least quarterly to coordinate special services, such as for black history and women's history months. If you meet monthly, you can plan the themes for each month's services as well as enlist the talents of the congregation, especially writers and artists. The committee could be made up of representatives from each of the congregation's standing committees or just of interested individuals.

Each member of the worship committee will, of course, contribute thoughts and insights. A member of each standing committee could be asked to coordinate his or her committee's involvement in worship, either in preparing liturgical materials or in leading the service. Worship committee members could pull the prepared pieces together into a service. In addition, a pool of creative writers and artists could meet weekly, or as needed, to create something entirely new for worship.

General committee guidelines may be summarized as follows:

1. Plan ahead. Allow enough time to gather resources, enlist people's help, and do some creative thinking before the week leading up to the service.

2. Set a specific theme for each service. In this way, everyone working on the different parts of the service can focus on a common image. One person coordinates the coming together of each service's pieces.

3. Involve the laity in worship. For example, start a lay reader program for Sunday scripture reading. Train laypersons to be worship leaders, handling everything but the sermon and pastoral prayer. Involve a variety of the arts in worship: music, creative writing, plays and skits, children's sermons, paintings, drawings, banners, paraments, flowers, candles, liturgical dance, home-baked bread for communion. Encourage members of the congregation to write liturgies and prayers for worship, either weekly or seasonally. Members could write Advent and lenten meditation books of stories and reflections on set themes.

4. Seek congregational feedback. Survey congregational responses to worship. Ask what parts of the service were most meaningful and which parts seemed tacked on.

5. Create a congregational statement on language. Let your members know what you are trying to accomplish through language, and be sure that everyone who speaks at church functions is aware of, and honors, the congregation's stand on language. (For guidelines, see chapter 2.)

6. Provide updates and promotions in the church newsletter.

Parts of a Worship Service

It is not necessary that any service have all of the elements discussed below or even that the parts be readily identifiable. Services of worship should be seamless, and one part should flow smoothly from the previous one. Before the advent of office copiers, the only parts of the service that were identified were the numbers of the hymns to be sung; these were displayed on a board at the front of the sanctuary. Although pastors in those days undoubtedly had services planned out, in the absence of bulletins for the congregation to follow it was easy to make changes if more time was needed for prayer, singing, or confession. Special services could also emphasize one aspect of worship and leave some parts out.

The usual parts of the worship service are as follows:

Words of meditation: These words help worshipers to slow their minds down after rushing to get to church, and assist in focusing on worship and the matters to come in the service.

Musical prelude: Music prepares the heart and the imagination to center on worship.

Announcements: As worship provides the main opportunity for the members of the congregation to gather, this is an appropriate time to share important announcements and schedule changes before the flow of worship begins. Keep announcements short. Some congregations make announcements before the prelude.

Procession: This is a visual way of saying to all gathered that worship is now beginning. Processing in an object, such as the Bible, signals the congregation to pay attention to it.

Call to worship: This is an act of praise or thanksgiving that can also introduce the theme of the service. It should be brief; it should not be a mini-sermon.

Passing the peace: Some people like to come to Sunday worship and be quiet with their thoughts. Others like to chat before the service. This time allows all congregants a chance to interact and greet one another as sisters and brothers in faith and to introduce themselves to people they don't know.

Hymns: To stand and physically sing involves the body in worship and unites the congregation in a common activity. This is often the laity's only physical activity in worship, although some congregations do kneel for prayer, come forward for communion, and sway to the music.

General prayers: These address a wide range of topics, but they all verbalize the concerns of our hearts.

Litany/liturgy: Responsive readings are designed to lay the groundwork and raise questions for the sermon to answer later.

Children's story: Most of the service is written with adults in mind. This time speaks to children of their concerns and uses language and images that they understand. Sometimes, if the story has the same theme as the sermon, its brevity helps adults figure out the point of the sermon.

Sermon: Sermons serve a variety of purposes. Some are designed to inspire, some to instruct on matters of faith or doctrine, some to convince by weight of argument. Usually scripture is the starting point.

Offering: This is a time for returning or committing to God a part of what one has received in terms of money, time, and skills.

Communion, or Eucharist: Every time we take communion, we renew our vow to follow God in all matters. By taking communion together, we affirm our commitment to help one another on this journey.

Pastoral prayer: This prayer gathers the congregation's concerns, and the pastor, in an official role, offers them up to God. It is a time of sharing our concerns with one another and listening together for God's response.

Recessional: This is the signal that our joint worship has ended. The drama of this liturgy is over, to be taken home and fleshed out through our lives until we come back together as a congregation next week.

Postlude: This is a time to let the details and feelings of the service settle into us so that we don't forget what has happened here in our postservice rush to talk to those we haven't seen recently.

Writing from Scripture

When a group wants to write about any scriptural passage, they should first read through it together. Jot down for future reference (perhaps on a chalkboard up front) all the images, thoughts, and concerns that arise. If the group is only writing on one passage, you may want to identify several aspects to a theme within the passage and have people break up into groups to work on each of them. Pieces written around a common theme that have different tones can create breadth and depth in a worship service. For example, in one place, you can talk about the positives of aggressive faith; in another, you can bring up the negatives. If you are working on several passages that will cover a number of Sundays—say, the weeks of Advent—you may want to identify four major themes in all the scriptures for Advent and see how they are linked before you begin to write.

The written material may take the form of anything you can create: hymns, lyrics, prayers, poetry, short stories, drawings, memories, dialogues, responsive readings, and litanies are but a few examples. Possibilities are only limited by your imagination and skills.

Example of Brainstorming on Scripture

Year C, First Sunday in Lent
Luke 4:1–13 In writing about this passage, which describes Jesus' temptation in the wilderness, some themes to consider are:

- Jesus was tempted; what are my temptations?
- Discuss the types of temptation: food, power, glory.
- It was the devil who tempted Jesus.
- Discuss angels and their existence.
- Is saying yes to the devil a means to a greater end?
- What does tempting God mean?
- Discuss Jesus' responses: won't follow devil for bread that doesn't last; can't worship devil, only God; can't tempt God because . . .
- What can be said about the existence of evil?
- Does God allow evil? Does God will evil? Can God control evil?
- What is temptation's hold on one who is full of the Holy Spirit?

- Is being full of the Spirit the same as being filled with the breath of God, mentioned in Genesis?
- How does Ruah/Sophia relate to Pneuma?
- What is the significance of forty days?
- Jesus had no food for forty days. Was he really human?
- Do you feel like you are lost in a wilderness every day?
- Offer a personal account of actually being lost.
- Discuss the hard conditions of life nowadays and in the past.
- Discuss the theology of inclusive language: "Child of God" vs. "Son of God."
- Was the phrase "until the opportune time" in the original text, or was it added later in light of the crucifixion?

Seasonal Meditation Books

Meditation books for Advent and Lent often focus principally on encouraging people to pray each day, since this is often a missing element in people's lives. A secondary focus is on educating readers on some matter of belief.

What should be included in seasonal meditation books? Because they are compilations of pieces contributed by congregation members, they include everything important to the individual contributors. A submission in which the writer takes a strong stand should be included in the book because that writer is a member of the congregation and deserves to be heard, as long as the material is presented in a responsible way and is on the assigned theme. A book that includes only what everyone agrees with will be so bland that no one will read it. Aim for a variety of distinctive perspectives on a topic that encourages each reader to think, reflect, probe his or her faith, and come up with conclusions.

What Are the Goals of a Meditation Book?

A meditation book is designed to accomplish many goals. It encourages daily, personal spirituality. It fosters in the reader a sense that although individuals may be praying by themselves during the week, they are doing so as a community. It conveys the sense that others are praying at the same time and praying throughout the day. This expands the church beyond the sanctuary to include all the territory between the homes of the members of the community, and beyond the Sunday hour to include all time. A meditation book offers a place where people's talents can be used: writing, drawing, editing, layout, printing, organizing, and the like. It furthers the congregation's understanding of itself through personal statements of faith and struggles, through expressions of different opinions and values, and through sharing the cross-cultural resources of its members.

A meditation book moves the congregation and its individual members into new ministries by recognizing needs within the congregation, awareness of community needs, and needs and resources from around the world.

What Is Required for a Meditation Book?

Writing a meditation book requires a committee to work with the pastor in deciding the book's overall theme and various subthemes. It is the committee's job—beginning as much as a year in advance of publication—to request, gather, and review materials submitted by members of the congregation.

A meditation book also requires an editor. It is the editor's job to work with writers and artists in reworking their material, either to aid understanding or to fit the allotted space or theme. The editor weaves the submissions together so that they flow and build upon one another, and writes the introductions and transition pieces.

An essential requirement of the meditation book is submissions. Original material is always best, because you want the congregation to share its stories. Published material should be used sparingly and always with attribution.

At least four months before you intend to distribute the book, place an item in the church newsletter so that people will have time to think about the themes. Two months ahead of publication, send out the call for submissions and ask that they be in the church office in a month. This will then give you a month to pull everything together and get it printed on time.

To generate submissions, it may be useful to sponsor a writing workshop in conjunction with a church arts Saturday workshop. For Advent, this could be in late October or early November. Some of the artists and craftspeople could offer suggestions, perhaps even write a description of the meaning behind their work (for example, what sewing religious symbols on paraments means to them). Writers may be inspired by the banners and other artwork being made.

Sunday-school assignments are also helpful in generating submissions. On one Sunday, the children could read the scripture to be used in Advent and offer their perspectives. Their words can be presented in a running dialogue, as is done in *The Gospel in Solentiname.*

Contact specific individuals from whom you want material. Some busy people often just need to be reminded and pushed to write something. Others, who don't think they have anything to say, come up with wonderful insights. Diligence here is often rewarded.

Organize a weekly workshop for people who want to learn to write better. Discuss and write about one theme per week. This workshop should focus on learning to write better and more creatively as much as on producing something usable. Material developed in these sessions can also be used to enrich worship services.

Possible Themes for a Meditation Book

The theme for the meditation book may be drawn from the weekly lectionary scripture. It may reflect an overall theme that runs through the season's scripture, the pastor's preaching themes, or a study about some aspect of Christianity (for example, the Bible, sacraments, church history, theology, ministry, or worship). Other possible themes are the Prayer of Our Savior, the Beatitudes, the prophets, the Psalms, or concepts like time, justice, or discipleship. Dealing with time during Advent, for example, suggests all sorts of ideas: the ending of another year of memories, the eternal sense of endless time, or the sense that "there is just too little time during Christmas to get everything done." Study questions can be provided to spur reflection.

Monthly Theme Planning

When planning worship for a month in the future, it is helpful to look at a variety of matters. If your congregation follows the lectionary, first check out the assigned scripture passages. If your congregation doesn't use the lectionary, ask the preacher what scriptures will be used and what themes are planned. Take time to look at the historical dates and cultural events that will come up in the month. Find out what is going on in the local community that is important to the members of the congregation, and try to incorporate these matters into the services.

As an example of monthly theme planning, look at the period from October 1 to November 4, the eighteenth to twenty-second Sundays of Pentecost. The prophet passages in the lectionary readings for this month offer a possible theme: the cycle of humanity's relationship with God. In Hosea, God spoke to an unruly people, who had forgotten the ways of their ancestors and fallen into living a dissolute life. God stepped in and offered them continued freedom if they would simply return to God. Joel promised the Jewish people that if they would trust in God, God would bring them prosperity. Amos warned the newly prosperous people that God blessed them not so they could enjoy themselves but so they would be faithful to God; they still needed to do their duty to God by establishing justice in their society. By the time Micah came along, matters had deteriorated. The prophet accused the people of not only allowing injustice to go on but actually causing and profiting from it. In Habakkuk, matters had gotten so bad that a few of the faithful finally realized what they had done and cried out to God for redemption. God announced that the vision still waited, thus bringing us back around to the words of Hosea.

The themes of the lectionary readings for the period in our example are as follows:

Eighteenth Sunday of Pentecost (October 1)

> Hosea 11:1–11, God's tender love for Israel.
>
> Psalm 107:1–9, thanksgiving to a delivering God.
>
> 1 Timothy 2:1–7, prayer for people in high places.
>
> Luke 16:1–13, unjust steward; can't serve two bosses.

Nineteenth Sunday of Pentecost (October 8)

> Joel 2:23–30, promise of abundant harvest.
>
> Psalm 107:1, 33–43, thanksgiving to a delivering God.
>
> 1 Timothy 6:6–19, steadfastness and fidelity.
>
> Luke 16:19–31, rich person and Lazarus; can't serve two masters.

Twentieth Sunday of Pentecost (October 15)

> Amos 5:6–7, 10–15, warning to establish justice in the land.
>
> Psalm 101, a profession of integrity.
>
> 2 Timothy 1:1–14, share in the suffering of the gospel.
>
> Luke 17:5–10, wages of a servant; just doing one's duty.

Twenty-first Sunday of Pentecost (October 22)

> Micah 1:2; 2:1–10, people accused of evil and injustice.
>
> Psalm 26, a plea for vindication.
>
> 2 Timothy 2:8–15, Christians' relationship with Christ.
>
> Luke 17:11–19, ten healed of leprosy; faith takes care of us.

Twenty-second Sunday of Pentecost (October 29)

> Habakkuk 1:1–3; 2:1–4, cry to God for redemption.
>
> Psalm 119:137–144, the righteousness of God's law.
>
> 2 Timothy 3:14–4:5, follow the teachings and be faithful to ministry.
>
> Luke 18:1–8, parable about prayer; persist in asking for what you need.

Cultural Festivals

It is important for congregations to celebrate the cultural diversity of their members. Observances can be planned for dates of historical significance throughout the year, or one month can be chosen to cover the whole range, with each week devoted to a different culture. Some cultures, like Hispanic American, have a specific month designated during the year.

If your congregation is made up of people only of European descent, you might, for example, divide the Sundays of one month among German, British, French, and Scandinavian cultures. If your members are all of African descent, you might divide the month into geographical areas of Africa.

Even if the membership of your congregation isn't multicultural, sharing with different cultural groups and engaging in interfaith discussions can bring new insights into your faith and seasonal traditions. The various cultural history months are a wonderful time to invite speakers and to share in joint worship services with other cultural groups. For example, an increasing number of churches are allowing Native American groups to set up sweat lodges on their property. This interaction, as well as sharing in sweat lodge activities, has deepened the prayer life of the welcoming congregations. Lists of suggested monthly cultural celebrations are given in the appendix at the end of this book.

October is a good month for celebrating the gifts of diversity as many congregations also celebrate the gifts of the summer harvest just concluding. For each Sunday of this special month, you might want to focus on a different culture each week or on a different art form as expressed through all the cultures. The first Sunday could be weaving from different cultures. The second Sunday could be pottery, painting, or poetry, and so on.

As an example, let us look at Worldwide Communion Sunday (October 1). Historical and cultural events commemorated this week include:

October 1. Yosemite National Park founded, 1890; World Habitat Day; Mohammed born, 570 C.E.

October 2. M. Gandhi born, 1869

October 4. Francis of Assisi dies, 1226; Yom Kippur

October 5. Tecumseh (Shawnee) dies, 1813

October 6. W. Tyndale dies, 1536

October 7. Toni Morrison wins Nobel Prize for Literature, 1993

Possible themes for the week include interdenominational communion, spirituality in nature, Habitat for Humanity (affordable housing), Christianity and Islam, Gandhi and peace, Saint Francis and the blessing of pets, animal testing, Tyndale and the Bible.

A congregational confession and healing service could be held in observance of Yom Kippur, the Feast of the Atonement. Celebrated on the tenth of *Tishri* (September/October), Yom Kippur ends the Ten Days of Repentance begun on Rosh Hashanah. Ceremonies include fasting and mourning, admitting mistakes, and seeking forgiveness for personal, congregational, and community transgressions. In ancient times, the observance was concluded by transferring the people's sins onto a scapegoat, which was released in the desert. At the end of the day, a celebration takes place.

Visual Ideas

Everything put in the sanctuary for worship should be thought through, especially what has been visible in the sanctuary for generations. This includes what is bolted down and cannot be moved: pews, tables, walls, lecterns, and pulpits.

Experiment with movable furniture. Move chairs, pews, and tables to different places, or turn them to face a different direction. This is particularly effective when the change enhances a service with a special theme.

Place visual displays on things that cannot be moved. What does its surface lend itself to? What would fit perfectly on a pillar? What kind of an object would enhance the piano top? Candles and flowers are objects common to most churches. Also consider banners, pottery, sculpture, and other works of art made by members of the community.

Enhance familiar objects by showing them in a new way. For example, carved wood reliefs that no one notices can be highlighted by tiny lights for special occasions to show them off or to create shadow effects.

Specific Items

Candles: Vary sizes, types, colors, holders, arrangements, even scents.

Paraments: Have different groups sew, weave, and tie-dye new ones for special occasions; incorporate theological symbols. Hang colorful banners from the walls, ceilings, or rafters.

Vestments and stoles: Sew new ones, try sashes, match designs or colors with what is on the banners.

Wall displays: On large, bare walls, hang artwork, paintings, drawings, quilts, or use the space to display poems or other writings by the congregation. For Black History Month, you could display examples of poetry written by African American authors throughout the centuries.

Movement: Use different kinds of processions and dancing to create visual flows of motion and energy. Fans can be used to create motion in displays.

2

~~

The Language of Worship in a Multicultural Setting

General Considerations

In worship, we aim to avoid an atmosphere where language gets in the way, where people feel confused about new words, guilty about using language they grew up with, or angry over words and images that either exclude or include. In most cases, people are not consciously trying to be sexist, exclusive, or hurtful when they use words that end up causing distress. We need to view concerns about language and the changes they bring not as negative restrictions but as positive affirmations of what we believe and as opportunities to learn more about one another's faith.

When creating worship in a multicultural setting, there are two concerns: (1) the language of worship itself and (2) this language in a multicultural setting.

The goal of worship is to move worshipers into the presence of God and have them experience something more about God and the community of faith. We come to worship to be comforted, healed, and challenged. We come to celebrate and be renewed. The language we use should facilitate this for everyone present. It should not be distracting. Too often, if we were to take all the words out of our services, we would have little left. We do not want people to feel guilty about using the language they grew up with; nor do we want them to stagnate in this language or be confused by new language that is introduced.

Language is not simple, and religious language has the additional complication of addressing an omnipotent being (with a measure of self-interest and guilt tossed in to gum up our best intentions). Most worshipers feel qualified to act as linguists, and they criticize the words we use because it is *their* experiences we are talking about. Who better to know what words are right for them than they themselves? Yet worship is a communal event, and we need to craft a common language that we all can use.

Words

Words name something or someone. They give ideas and feelings form. They provide handles for understanding what is being discussed. Yet as each word brings together many pieces of information, by saying that something is *this,* we are also saying that it is not *that.* Therefore, it is important to be intentional and precise about our worship language. What is said in worship takes on an aura of being "official," and sometimes those who have chosen the words are still struggling to get them right.

Words have a mystery and a creative force to them. Because we often hear words before we see them, there is meaning in how they sound—a blending of sound and sense. The use of alliteration, onomatopoeia, and repetition recalls the time before written language when spoken words preserved traditions and carried stories from one generation to the next. Words needed to be chosen carefully so that their sounds would aid the people's memory. Words have a cadence that echoes the rhythms of life. Sometimes the sounds of words are as uplifting as their meanings. Read the beginning of the Gospel of John and listen to its sounds. Within those words live a rhythm and an imagery that transcend the particulars of the words.

Words do not mean what the dictionaries say. They exist only as we have experienced them, by how they were used where we grew up, and by the culture around us. So it's not surprising that we don't all mean the same thing when we use the same words. While it may make perfect sense to Norwegians to pray that their sins be washed as white as snow, it makes considerably less sense to people who have never seen snow or who live in large cities where the snow is dirty.

When someone prays "God, keep us warm when it's cold outside," some of us are thinking about being uncomfortable, while others are thinking about freezing to death. It's the same word but with vastly different meanings. In Wisconsin everyone can talk about when "cool" ends and "cold" begins, although people who move in from out of state sometimes have to be properly instructed.

By living in community, we hear one another's stories and learn how to interpret the meaning behind the words. This is especially important in multicultural communities. Because we care about one another, we have a desire to speak precisely and use words responsibly.

We are also discovering that the words we use in church are not always faithful to our beliefs, especially in the old hymns. Words change their meanings over time. They fall into disuse and then come back meaning something completely different. For example, in the King James Version, "to let" meant to prevent someone from doing something. Today this phrase means "to allow"—the opposite of its earlier meaning.

Inclusiveness and Multiculturalism

There is a growing awareness of the sexism, racism, and culturalism inherent in our language, of values put on words that they were never intended to carry. We have inherited a religious language that uses masculine metaphors and pronouns as if they were neutral. Yet if our language excludes women or any cultural group, we are in effect saying that these people are not welcome in worship, that they are outside the love of God. If our worship is open to all who profess faith in Jesus Christ, then our worship language must also be open and not exclude. To sing "O brother man, fold to thy heart thy brother" in a setting where women and men are present is a problem. "Brother" does not include "sister," and "man" no longer means "male and female."

Although using language that includes both men and women is a concern that has been around for more than a century, inclusive language goes beyond this to value all cultures and all races. Persons not mentioned and sensibilities not taken into account cease to exist. The gospel mandates full equality for all human beings, and the gospel travels on the words we use.

Metaphors: Limitations of Words in Describing Abstract Concepts

Language used in religious settings is not simple. There are layers of meaning beneath layers. We try to describe and explain the reality and nature of God by using words, even though words always fall short.

Metaphors and similes are useful when trying to compare our experiences, which we know something about, to the nature of God: "God is like the dawn, bringing warmth to the world," and "God is my friend, always there when I need someone." We even attempt to describe abstract, philosophical concepts with labels: "God is truth." This is a fine statement, but whose truth? "God is love." What kind of love? Are we talking about all kinds today or just one kind?

By using similes and metaphors we get closer to reality. But if similes are overused, they too easily slide into becoming metaphors. We start off by saying "God rules like the king of a nation," and we end up saying: "God is king," with a castle and fortified walls and a moat. Overused metaphors become mistaken for reality.

Sometimes we end up using one metaphor for God so much that it creates a distorted picture of God's nature: too much talking about God as conquering King, and we find ourselves going off on crusades; too much of supreme Judge, and we re-create the Mosaic code with laws for everything; too much of heavenly Father, and we imagine someone who is absent most of the time doing work more important than being with us. Although handy, it is not accurate to speak of any Person of the Trinity as "he" or "she." But rather than discard gender-based metaphors altogether, we can renovate them. Mix them together. Look to God as Friend, Counselor, Creator, as Mother and as Father. Use images from nature—strong Wind, mighty Bear, sparkling Light, solid Rock.

Diversity of Images

We can be lazy when describing God. We like to use terms that keep God locked up at a distance and out of our day-to-day lives, concepts like almighty, eternal, and omniscient.

At times, we do use images that are more down-to-earth, such as Jesus the shepherd. Yet this is not fail-safe, because of people's different experiences. The image of a shepherd, for example, doesn't do much for me. I grew up in Wisconsin where there are a great many cows but not many sheep. Historically, I know it was significant. It still conjures up images of care, although the biblical stories never seem to mention that sheep are dirty, smelly animals. But talk about "God of the farmlands," or "God who hikes the mountain trails," and I am touched where my heart lives.

The point is not to lock God into one mode of being. We need to use as many images as we can when describing God, especially images that are part of our daily lives. We have endless possibilities for being creative: God of the snowy peaks, God who dances and laughs, Weaver God, Artist God, Companion, Friend, Teacher.

Language should not limit us in how we think about God. Language should challenge us to see, understand, and feel more of the full diversity of God's being. We need to be moved in the deepest parts of our being, and the images we use in language are a doorway into this world.

Rituals: The Patterns of Words

Traditions of words with a long history of meaning create a sense of devotion around them. They take on an aura of holiness. Hearing them said in just the right way seems to recreate special memories. This is not to be taken lightly, because this is the essence of ritual. There is a need in us to reclaim and explore the ancient rhythms and insights as well as to proclaim the new ones that break open the symbols of faith for our time. Sometimes the most important meaning to the words we speak is not in the words themselves but in the ritual of the congregation's rising and speaking these words together in a confession of belief.

In some denominations, set liturgies are used every week. If based on the Bible, these can be a great teaching device. If they blend scripture, prayer, and hymns in a flowing combination, the experience can be profound. Yet set liturgies can also be stifling. If there is only one liturgy for all the weeks of Advent, for example, our attention and imagination are asleep by the third or fourth week. Sometimes the pattern of words becomes the message; set forms can take on the negative sense of ritual and replace meaning with empty structure. This may lead people to think that, by proper observance of the form, they can force God to do their bidding because they have said the right words in the correct way at the proper time.

It is helpful to vary the standard forms just to keep people alert. For example, the familiar call to worship, "Let us focus our hearts and minds," could be replaced for one week with the exclamation "Isn't it great to be alive!" In the responsive reading, rather than always alternating lines between the leader and the congregation, a reader up front could be added to read the third lines, a reader on the side for the fourth, and maybe someone in the balcony for the occasional fifth. The familiar twenty-minute sermon in the middle of the service could be varied by starting the service with the sermon or ending with it. Now and then, the sermon could last only five minutes. Instead of always using three examples in the sermon, select one solid example that will stick in people's minds. Make the benediction a challenge instead of a blessing, or ask the congregation to devise their own benediction based on what has happened in the service.

Sometimes the pattern of words is as important as the words themselves because they catch us, wrap us up in their energy, and carry us to another place. One preaching style—echoing the speech patterns in an oral society—starts with an image, divides it into three parts, expands each slightly by giving three examples in a rotating sequence; this style features a cadence that builds in tempo and emotion until the whole congregation is caught up both in mind and body and swept away.

Sometimes we never hear the specific words in a service because the service just flows and carries us along like a boat floating down a river. On Communion Sunday, the parts of the service prepare us to receive the elements; afterward, while we may not be able to remember a single word that was said, we know that we have been changed. The language of the service, the ritual, has carried us.

Limnality

Ritual takes us to the edges of our lives, to the places where something new is happening, where movement is not locked down by habit or tradition. This is the place of limnality, where understanding and mystery touch. It is where prayer lives. Here we are willing to listen and are open to being guided and challenged; here we are empty and await with open arms and hearts whatever God may send our way.

In these special times, when we are open to all possibilities, we are able to experience what is simply here—the ontological flash, the "aha!" of insight and deep freedom. Here symbols acquire new meanings. Here the inadequacy of language is most evident, for we realize that perhaps only a single phrase in the thousands of words used in today's worship service has struck home and changed our perspective forever. One Sunday, as Frederick Buechner was listening to the service, he heard the pastor say, "We are saved by laughter." Suddenly the gates of faith opened up to him, and his life was changed.

Scripture/Bible Translations

Every translation of the Bible offers something that other translations do not. The King James Version has poetic beauty. The New Revised Standard Version is up to date with biblical scholarship; it is inclusive of all people when the text is inclusive.

It is good to use different translations from time to time because of what they have to offer, especially since most of us cannot read the Bible's original languages—Greek, Hebrew, and Aramaic. Some of the original words do not translate easily into English, especially when abstract concepts are involved, and the various translations use different words to try to express these meanings.

It is especially helpful to consult a different translation for those passages that we know by heart in one translation. By reading slightly different words, old passages may become not just a comfort but a challenge again. They may seem as fresh as when we first read them. We are also able to pick up the various nuances that the words carry, nuances that can lead us to greater appreciation of the diversity of God's activity in the world.

Hymn Lyrics

With psalms and chants, spirituals and chorales, we sing our faith. The words of our hymns also shape us in subtle ways; therefore, they need to be chosen carefully. Since many hymns were written before inclusive language became a concern, we are faced with a dilemma. Do we not sing those verses and hymns that exclude? Do we change the pronouns to be inclusive? Do we rewrite concepts to fit our values? Or do we write entirely new lyrics or entirely new hymns?

Some needed changes are easy, especially if we know the writer was trying to be inclusive. Modifying a word here or a phrase there to bring it into line with current linguistic practices, such as changing "mankind" to "people" is acceptable as long the rhythm of the music is not disturbed. The intent is not to jar the listener but to weave the changes in seamlessly and maintain the flow of the hymn's meter and rhyme. If many words are being modified, and certainly if the meaning is being altered, it is more respectful to write a new verse and attribute authorship accordingly. Lavon Baylor, Ruth Duck, Jane Parker Huber, Brian Wren, and other current hymn writers are doing this as well as writing new music for old lyrics. Martin Luther also did this; by writing new words to beer-hall tunes and then playing the results in church, he created songs we have come to treasure, like "A Mighty Fortress Is Our God."

Sometimes hymns are important not because they are great hymns but because they have been situationally important. Some people feel that a certain hymn must be used at funerals because, where they grew up, that hymn was always used. Its ritual presence provides a strong reassurance that all is well. The music of hymns often transcends the power of reason. We need to be mindful of this. Some hymns—even those whose theology we disagree with—simply inspire great emotion in us. Others evoke haunting nightmares; for example, hymns written to military tunes may revive horrible war memories in some listeners.

There are powerful reasons to use new hymns in church. Christians continue to write them in response to God's movement in their lives, and we want to affirm this gift in our community. New hymns also address concerns that are specific to our times.

Guidelines to Inclusiveness

Be mindful whenever using terms that imply gender, especially for things or entities that do not have gender. If a church is always a "she," then a system is set up in which God is always a "he," and the "he" is set up as always being in control taking care of the "shes"—even in human situations. Be aware of sexism that says only males or only females can do some activity well.

Avoid words or images that are offensive to others. This does not mean that you should not challenge people to experience new images that may initially make them uneasy.

Be contemporary in language without being faddish. Choose your words carefully.

Try not to use words or images that exclude. If you do, balance the presentation with other words and images. For example, if you use "Father" to refer to God in some of God's aspects, use "Mother" to refer to God elsewhere in the service. Also balance imagery regarding other dualities in society, such as male/female, rich/poor, single/married, old/young, and the like. Avoid racism, culturalism, and classism in your language; be aware of the groups you are including and excluding. If your language excludes women (or men) or any minority group, you are in effect saying that those people are not welcome in worship.

Be careful when attaching judgment to colors. We've inherited set values to some colors. For example, black/dark/night are often equated with evil; white/light/day often convey images of goodness. To counteract prejudicial images, balance color imagery and use colors in a context opposite to their usual ones.

Be sensitive to human relationships. Don't hold up the mother/father/two children image of the family as the only model. It's not. The church also needs to speak of couples (both heterosexual and homosexual), families without children, single-parent families, extended families, widowed persons, and so forth. The key value here is commitment in a caring relationship.

Use as many images as possible, from as many sources as you can. By doing so, you will engage the hearts and minds of your people in worship.

A multicultural community offers a wealth of images that single-culture communities do not provide. We must tap into this rich resource. The more images we use, the closer we get to a full picture of God.

Be aware of language that uses words of violence and force rather than words of cooperation and love to get its message across. Christians do not work on the principle that the ends justify the means (to which the lessons of the Inquisition will attest). Images such as "O God, rip the sin from our lives!" "Shoot a bullet of love into our resistant hearts!" "Let us go and make people believe in Christ" are not particularly helpful, although their intent may be good. These images convey a belief that God forces people to believe, that free will is not a reality, that we can do what we want and God will have to save us in due time. It also gives us permission to do violence to people if we do it for their own good. The language of war and violence is not appropriate for a people of peace.

The Challenge

We need to move beyond nondiscriminatory language to language that emancipates. We are beginning to realize that any words we use to talk about God are only metaphors and that the words we use reflect our values.

Each generation needs to discover a vernacular way of declaring the liberating gospel, to find the words that capture and express its own feelings and thoughts, and this always involves a time of awkwardness. Sacred speech is not self-evident. The words that say so much to one generation do not automatically speak to all generations.

Most people in any congregation hold the same basic beliefs. What often separates them and causes conflict is an inability to talk about their faith in words that others understand. Our worship addresses God, but it also represents one place where we can learn a common language.

We should come away from worship with our hearts excited, our tongues rolling with phrases, our eyes filled with images, and our minds focused on thoughts that heal, challenge, and guide. Liturgy is truly the work of the people of God, for our worship guides our actions through the week as we seek to be God's hands in the world. Those who choose the words used in worship need to remember that although words can lead us to the promised land, they cannot enter it with us. Words only lead us to the silence that is beyond words. Then we must step forward by ourselves and stand mute before God.

Part Two

Seasons of the Church Year

3

Advent, Christmas, and Epiphany

December is a time for celebrating life in the Northern Hemisphere: a time to bring out some of the good harvest that came from the fields this year; a time when the earth begins to move back toward the sun, promising longer days of sunlight and warmth; a time to evaluate the past year and to prepare for what is to come. People in many cultures have created traditions of celebrations for this month: Hanukkah, *Las Posadas,* the winter solstice, Christmas, Kwanzaa, and the New Year.

The secular and the sacred are often mixed together at this time of year, and this tends to scatter our focus. But would Christmas for Christians be the same without tinsel and Santa Claus? Would we miss office Christmas parties and television Christmas specials? For some, it is a time of renewal, a time to stop what one is doing and take stock of life: Am I who I want to be? Am I doing what I set out to do? It is a time of mending fences with people, of recovenanting with God, of saying "yes" again to the goodness that is available in life. Christmas has become a time of family gatherings, of strengthening the bonds that exist, and feeling the tension of bonds that are frayed or fraying.

This long period of celebration offers modern Christians, many of whom have forgotten much of their cultural heritage, an opportunity to reclaim some of their rich traditions. It also offers a time of "coming home" for those who have been rejected by their families or frozen out of society's rituals because of who they are. For them, Christmas is a time of gathering with friends as a substitute for their families of origin.

Christians first celebrated the birth of Jesus on January 6 and called it "Epiphany" because God was revealing something new. Not until 325 C.E., in another part of the world, did December 25 become the date for celebrating Jesus' birth. The winter solstice festival was traditionally held on that day, and church officials wanted to replace it with a Christian celebration. The twelve days of Christmas, also known as "Christmastide," is the period from the new feast day (December 25) to the old feast day (January 6). In many Latin American countries, January 6 is the day for giving presents.

Advent is the period leading up to Christmas and marks the start of the church year. It began in France as a six-week season of preparation for baptism. In the sixth century, this was shortened to the four Sundays before Christmas, beginning on the Sunday nearest Saint Andrew's Day, November 30. The focus switched to being a preparation for the birth of Jesus. Advent today is a period of quiet waiting, anticipation, and sometimes fasting before the celebration begins on the evening of December 24. Advent traditions vary from place to place, depending upon the culture.

The colors of the season are violet, purple, and blue. Some churches use rose as the color on the third Sunday because of the lighter tone to the traditional reading on that day (Phil. 4:4: "Rejoice in God"). Some of the more popular traditions include the use of Advent wreaths, logs, calendars, stars, and the placing of lights in windows.

Advent is a season of preparing for the birth of Jesus into the world and for a rebirth in our lives. It is a time of awe and wonder, a time of receiving the good news so deeply into our hearts, minds, and souls that we become more Christlike. It is a time of offering the joy and hope we feel to a world that so desperately needs the investment and involvement of ourselves. Advent also gives us a hint of what is to come in Jesus' life. Some traditions place a heavy emphasis on self-examination and repentance, on preparing for the second coming, when Christ will come in judgment. This adds a somber note to the birthday festivities, and sometimes we simply need to celebrate.

During the Christmas season, the world remembers the incarnation of Christ, God's taking on of human form. The Christmas season includes a number of special days. These honor Saint Stephen, the first Christian martyr; Saint John, the apostle and evangelist; and the holy innocents killed in Bethlehem because of Jesus' birth. The color for the season is white.

Worship services on Christmas Eve and Christmas Day vary. Some churches have a "Lessons and Carols" service early on Christmas Eve, designed for families with young children. Others hold a more liturgical service around midnight. Some meet on Christmas Day for their main Christmas service.

Epiphany was originally an Eastern festival that celebrated both the incarnation and the baptism of Jesus on January 6. In the West, the focus came to be on the arrival of the Magi (the three kings). The baptism of Jesus is then observed on the Sunday following Epiphany.

Many cultures have their own traditional ways of celebrating Advent, Christmas, and Epiphany. In Hispanic traditions, festivities generally begin on December 16 and end on January 6. The nine days preceding Christmas represent the nine months that Mary was pregnant with Jesus. On each of these days, the drama of *Las Posadas* (the inns) is enacted on the city streets. This daily drama tells the story of Joseph and Mary looking for a place to stay in Bethlehem and being repeatedly turned away.

After the celebrations of Christmas Eve and Christmas Day slow down, the festivities of *Los Pastores* (the shepherds) are held in early January. This folk drama, which depicts the shepherds' travel to Bethlehem to see the Christ child, actually is a means of teaching Bible stories and lessons of faith. The arrival of the Magi is celebrated on January 6.

In Mexico the first two weekends in December are the time of the *Fiesta de las Luminarias,* the lighting of the Holy Family's way to Bethlehem, often illustrated by lining walkways with candles inside paper bags filled with sand. December 12 is also celebrated in Mexico as the day the Virgin of Guadalupe appeared.

Many cultures use traditional objects for celebrating Advent, Christmas, and Epiphany. These include:

Advent calendar: This is generally a Christmas scene printed on cardboard, with punch-out windows scattered around the picture. One window is opened each day to reveal another picture underneath— something symbolic of Christmas or the Christmas story, like an ornament or presents.

Advent crèche/putz scene: This grouping of figurines depicts either the scene in the manger or the entire nativity story, complete with hillsides, sheep, camels, deserts, a moving star, and so on. Some churches read scripture and sing hymns while tiny spotlights follow the course of the narration on the putz. (See the Christmas putz story that appears later in this chapter.)

Advent cross: The Tau cross, which is in the shape of a T, is said to look like the staff Moses put up for healing. It has come to symbolize the birth of Jesus as the great healer.

Advent log: Involving the same symbolism as the Advent wreath, the log has a candle for each Sunday of Advent. These candles are lined up in a row instead of in a circle.

Advent rose: This wild rose blooms in Palestine at the same time each year. It is used to symbolize the faithfulness of God in keeping the promise to send a Savior.

Advent star: This is a three-dimensional star made out of paper points and illuminated from the inside by an electric bulb. The Moravians began making these in the 1850s, and now they are used by Christians around the world. They generally range in size from one-foot-tall models used in homes to five-foot versions used in church sanctuaries.

Advent wreath: This is a ring of evergreens on which are placed four purple candles (or three purple candles and one rose-colored one); a fifth candle, white, is placed in the center. The circular shape of the wreath stands for the unending love of God. The evergreens (or holly and laurel) represent the immortality and new life found in Christ. The light of the candles reminds us of Jesus, the Light of the world. Purple has always been considered a royal color and symbolizes the coming sovereignty of Jesus. Purple, or violet, also represents our humility. Sometimes churches assign each candle a specific meaning within a theme. One grouping includes the prophets, shepherds, angels, and Magi. Another grouping includes hope, peace, love, and joy. On Christmas Day, the white Christ candle in the center of the wreath is lit, representing the perfection of Christ.

Christmas tree: Although the use of evergreens was used by pre-Christians to stand for everlasting life, it was adopted by Christians to symbolize the life found in Christ.

Jesse tree: This is a tree hung with emblems representing the genealogy of Jesus. Often the emblems are made out of wood.

Poinsettia: According to one story, a young Mexican girl wanted to give a present to baby Jesus. An angel told her to pick some green weeds along the road and present them to Jesus in the church. As she did so, the weeds turned into flame-red flowers.

Window lights: This tradition was adopted by the Moravians, who used beeswax candles. Putting lights in the windows of one's home signaled an openness to the Christ child and to travelers, inviting all to come in for something warm to drink.

The Sundays of Advent

Advent Liturgics

WORDS OF PREPARATION

Join with us, Christ, in this hour of worship. Lift us out of the routine of our daily lives and set us up on your holy mountain. Let our worship come from our hearts, that it may be genuine. Let our praises for you leap from our mouths, that we may be alive with faith and joy. Make us fresh again!

CALL TO WORSHIP

Walking in the Light
Isaiah 2:1–5

One: What do you want from Christmas?
Many: We want this Christmas to be perfect.
One: How are you going to make that happen?

Many: We are going to go up on the mountain of God and learn God's ways. We will put away our drunkenness, quarrels, and addictions. We will beat our swords into plowshares.

One: It is time to become fully awake.

Many: It is time to walk in God's light.

Voices of Christmas: Repentance
Isaiah 11:1–10

One: Where are the voices that lead us to faith in Christ?

Many: In the wilderness where people like John the Baptist are calling out "Repent!"

One: Where are the voices that call us to justice and hope?

Many: In our streets, where people like Martin Luther King Jr. and Dorothy Day call into question the comfort of our lives.

One: The voices of repentance, the voices of justice. You hear the voices. What are you going to do?

Many: We are going to turn our lives around and live for Christ.

Healing and Forgiveness
Isaiah 35:1–10

One: Prepare the dry land of your hearts for the coming of Jesus!

Many: We hear the cry of the oppressed and the suffering.

One: Prepare the wilderness of your lives for deliverance!

Many: We feel the brokenness that is inside us.

One: Prepare for your dreams to be fulfilled!

Many: God will come down and live among people, and we will sing songs of freedom. We will bind up our aching knees, go to the people of all nations, and work for their liberation.

Fulfillment and Joy
Psalm 24

One: Do we feel like people who are full of joy and excitement?

Many: Do you mean like "Christmas people"?

One:	Do we feel closer to God because of the Christmas celebrations this year?
Many:	Are we supposed to?
One:	Who will be with Christ?
Many:	Those who have clean hands and pure hearts.
One:	What does that mean?
Many:	That those who want to be near God will be.
One:	Do you want this?
Many:	We do.
One:	Then let us worship and celebrate the pregnancy of a young woman and the coming fulfillment of all our dreams.

Watching
Psalm 130:6

One:	God calls us to watch, to stand on the city walls and see what is coming, as sentinels watch for the dawn. But what are we to watch for?
Many:	We're watching for the bus at Fourteenth and Broadway. We're watching for our children to come home. We're watching for the coming of Christ's power into the world and our lives, and opportunities for us to share this energy with others.
One:	Anything else?
Many:	We're watching for the signs of peace and justice in a world of much hardness and injustice. And we're watching our rulers to see if they see the signs of change.
One:	Is that all you watch?
Many:	We also watch television and see the struggles going on around the world. It leaves us feeling powerless, guilty, and sad to think that people can treat the rest of God's children with such hatred and violence.
One:	But watching for God is not the same as watching television.
Many:	So how do we watch with despair staring us in the face and not be overcome? How do we watch with feelings of powerlessness and still keep our hope?
One:	We do so by going out into the world and watching Christ move through our words and actions into the lives of others.

Waiting
2 Peter 3:8–15a

One: In anticipation we gather.

Many: With expectations we wait.

One: We gather to watch for the coming of the good news into our world and into our lives.

Many: We wait to see the fullness of God's vision.

One: O God, open the doors to our hearts that this year we may have room for the birth of Jesus.

Many: O God, as we marvel over all that you are doing, overwhelm us with so much wonder that words of praise spring forth from our lips!

One: In this time of waiting, let true worship begin in our hearts.

Many: Let our praises rise up to the heavens! Let our celebrations spread new hope over a tired world! Let us gather all our dreams and lives together and worship our God! Amen.

Witness
Psalm 24:3–5; Romans 1:1–7

One: We are all called to witness to God, yet there are a variety of ways in which we do this.

Many: We witness by believing that this birth really happened, by believing that what the Scriptures say about Jesus is true.

One: We witness by living lives that express our beliefs—living with clean hands, pure hearts, and by not committing our souls to what is false and temporary.

Many: We witness by sharing with others, through what we say and do, just how important Jesus' birth is to us.

One: As servants of God striving to be saints, we have agreed to live lives of great compassion and mercy, completely dedicated to the work of God.

Many: We need to take care, however we witness, that we do not let our good intentions get ahead of the Spirit's plans, for it is the Holy Spirit that touches the hearts of others.

Wonder
Exodus 15:11

One: Do we feel wonder anymore when we talk about the birth of Jesus? Do we have any sense of awe that God would decide to become human?

Many: We do find it hard to feel any wonder. Every few years science makes possible what we thought was impossible. But on the spiritual level, nothing seems to change.

One: So how do we recapture the wonder of this birth?

Many: By starting with this birth, and seeing where it leads.

Prepare
Baruch 5:1–9

One: Prepare the way! Level every mountain! Fill in every valley! Make the road smooth, for royalty is coming.

Many: What can we do? We don't own any machines big enough to move mountains. We have only shovels.

One: Then take your shovels to the roads that run through your lives. Smooth out the bumps. Fill in the potholes. Clear the brush that has grown up along the sides.

Many: We can do that. But what difference will it make?

One: The changes may seem small to you. But Christ isn't coming in a great presidential motorcade. Christ is coming on a bicycle, stopping here and there among us to chat, to share a meal, to borrow a warm coat for the night.

Many: We want Christ to dwell among us, so we will change our ways and care for those around us as if they were Christ.

One: Prepare the way this day for Christ's coming!

Rejoicing
Zephaniah 3; Philippians 4

One: Sing aloud, O daughter of Zion! Shout, O son of Israel! Rejoice and exalt with all your heart!

Many: God is in our midst! We shall fear disaster no more!

One: God will heal the infirm and gather the outcast!

Many: God will change our shame into praise!

One: You who suffer through no fault of your own; you who have trouble seeing, talking, hearing, and walking; you whose bodies don't fit society's ideals; you who don't feel completely understood or accepted; you whose interests and skills don't bring enough money to make you a "success"; you who respond with your hearts before your heads, and feel ashamed because of this; and all you who hold fast to God when so much of society says religion is irrelevant . . .

Many: For all of us who don't feel we measure up because of who we are and what we believe, and who have felt ashamed and suffered because of this . . .

One: For your perseverance and faith in matters greater and deeper than what can be seen, God will bring you home with joy, as hostages who return from captivity in a foreign country. Do not grow weary. Do not let your hearts grow weak, for God has come and is in our midst!

Peace
Luke 1:39–55

Reader 1: Mary treasured everything the shepherds said about Jesus but pondered how it was going to be possible.

Reader 2: "This child will establish a world of peace and justice, a world filled with righteousness!"

Many: This child? The one lying in the feeding bin?

Reader 1: This child, the one with humble beginnings.

Reader 2: "A child has been born for us! And the rod of the oppressor will be broken! The yoke of repression will be lifted!"

Many: It's been two thousand years since this child fulfilled the promises. Does this look like a world of peace?

Reader 1: At least now such a world of peace is possible.

Reader 2: "The people who live in a land of deep shadows have seen a great light!" And all who come after this child and believe become the child's hands, feet, and voice in this world.

Many: You mean us, the ones squirming in the pews?

Reader 1: If you take the first step, even a baby step, then all miracles become possible!

Many: Then so be it!

Reader 2: Amen!

CALL TO CONFESSION

We cannot come before God unless we are first honest with ourselves about who we are, about the mistakes we make, and how well or how poorly we care for others. In this spirit, let us offer our prayers to God.

UNISON PRAYERS

Holy Spirit, as we prepare ourselves this Advent, be with us and restrain us from trying to do everything. Kindle within us an unquenchable desire to be with you. Do we want to prepare? Do we want to start a serious walk of faith again? O Spirit, take that one thought of renewal within our many doubts and make it grow within us like the first light of dawn. Amen.

Spirit of the desert, the voice of John the Baptist shouting in the wilderness is not the voice we like to hear. After all, we've already repented once. Yet we sense that John knew repentance only goes so far. It's what we do afterward that develops the heart of faith. O God, grant us the courage to truly change and live out our convictions every day. Amen.

We are going to go up on your mountain, dear God. We are going to hear your words and learn your ways. We will take our actions and words that tear people down and turn them into what will tear down the walls that keep us from caring for one another. We will listen and learn. We will study and live your wisdom. Help us hike up your holy mountain!

Touchable God, will we feel like Christmas people this year? Will we want to affirm what is good in the world even in the midst of so much that doesn't seem to be going well? Are we ready to be open to people in a way that allows us to help one another get along? Can we let this Christmas be *this* Christmas, and not some Christmas from the past or one that exists only in our dreams? We're not sure. We feel confused so much of the time. We don't feel ready. What do we want this year? What are our expectations? O God, we have so many questions for you today. Help us settle our minds and listen to our hearts. Help us prepare to receive your joy without reservation.

Potter God, return us as clay to the potter to be re-formed, to have our excesses and accumulations taken off, to be refired in the kiln of your love. God of the rhythm that moves through creation, return us to our homes, to the places of our families' nurturing, that we may reclaim our dreams. Help us travel back to our spiritual homelands, to the tribes of our heritage, that we may bring the rhythms of their songs into our hearts. Amen.

Ubiquitous God, we wait for so many things. We are a needy people. We wait for you to teach us wisdom. We wait for you to show us how to walk humbly upon your way. We wait for you to help us with our personal problems and to administer justice in our often unjust world. Sometimes it seems that all we do is wait for matters to get better, and sometimes we become weary of waiting. Yet we believe, with Isaiah, that our waiting is almost over. The One who will bring light to our shadows, warmth to our cold, and hope to our future is about to be born. As we prepare for the birth this year, may we wait with a patience that is open to new ways. May we wait with a hope that is hard to tear down. May we wait upon the city walls through the solitude of the night and feel our hearts leap when we see the beginnings of dawn on the horizon. Amen.

Mother, we know you have appointed us to bring glad tidings to the afflicted, to proclaim the time of God's favor, to work so hard that we are called oaks of righteousness. Yet can we proclaim and do your word if we are not ourselves set free, or fed, or comforted? Give us the courage to comfort when we are in mourning, for then we will truly understand sadness and loss, and our words will come from the depths of our hearts. When we are hungry, let us feed others first, allowing those around us to see our needs and the opportunity to minister to us in your name. Thus we may know true hunger and true gratitude. Amen.

Eternal One beyond understanding, the deeper we move into your mystery by saying "yes" to your ways, the more we are amazed that your ways actually work! And the more we say "yes," the more we find we want to say "yes" in ways that are deeper and more encompassing. How mysterious and wonderful you are!

We are nervous, God, when we approach you with our needs. We feel we cannot come before you if we are not honest about ourselves. For some of us, the flame and glow of serving has grown dim, as with Moses in the wilderness once the burning bush was extinguished. Some of us have lost our way in the deserts of our lives. Our enthusiasm for the beauties of life has hardened into simple plans for survival. God, help us overcome our feelings of resignation. Help us feel again what it is that we believe, see again what waits in our dreams, and dream again of what we can do for you. Rekindle in us the passion for new life. Breathe upon our glowing embers and ignite our flame. This Advent, free us to love again. Amen (Luke 21:25–36).

Giver of gifts, we know we are not lacking in any spiritual gift, and yet we are not all on your journey of faith. Help us worry less about what's wrong with other people and focus more on being loving, hopeful, forgiving, and supportive. Let us remember all those who have died trying to bring mercy, healing, and faith to others: *[list their names].* For their witness, we give you thanks. Amen.

In the time to come, O Mother, in times of confusion and needing, in the stumbling of doubts and fears, as our relationships stretch and test their bonds, be present with your caring arms. Comfort and nurture us into fullness. Out of you comes this life, and only with you does it continue. O birthing Spirit, move us now with your rhythms!

WORDS OF ASSURANCE

God watches out over us when we are away from one another, protecting us, caring for us, guiding us. And if we stay faithful in our watching for God, we will see God's unexpected blessings all around us, as the shepherds did on that night long ago.

When we humble ourselves, God welcomes us. When we ask for help, God hears. God comforts the brokenhearted and guides those who have lost their way. God is with us.

As the rain falls to water the earth, as seeds grow to nourishing grain, God's Word will not return to God empty or unfulfilled. It will not return until our longing for God is filled.

BENEDICTIONS

Humility
1 Thessalonians 3:9–13

One:	Go and make a new beginning.
Many:	We ask for humility and trust.
One:	Go and deepen your life in the Holy Spirit.
Many:	We ask that we may see the spirit of Jesus Christ around us.
One:	Go with the love of Jesus and the power of the Spirit.
Many:	So be it. This service is ended. Let our service begin.

Hope
Phil. 1:3–11

One:	We have gathered in the name and spirit of Jesus Christ.
Many:	We have gathered as God's people, uniting our voices.
One:	Let us take, then, the promise of faith into the events of a new week.
Many:	Let us take, then, the compassion of Christ into the workings of our lives.
One:	Let us go as ministers of this church to serve God and love our neighbors with all the compassion and mercy we can muster.
Many:	Amen.

Advent Candle Readings

After the first Sunday in Advent, the previous candles are lit before the service begins. Only the new candle for that particular Sunday is lit during the reading.

FIRST SUNDAY IN ADVENT

> *Watch*
> *Mark 13:32–37*

Reader 1: "Beware, keep alert; for you do not know when the time will come. . . . Therefore, keep awake . . . or else you may be asleep when the Savior comes suddenly. And what I say to you I say to all: Keep awake."

Reader 2: We light our first Advent candle today to remind us to watch for Jesus. God has promised to send a Savior. But sometimes we become too busy and too distracted, and we forget to watch.

Reader 3: Let us pray. God, help us remember this candle throughout the coming week. May it remind us to stay alert and to watch for what is coming. Amen.

SECOND SUNDAY IN ADVENT

> *Wait*
> *Psalm 27:14*

Reader 1: "Wait for the Savior; be strong, and let your heart take courage; wait for the Savior."

Reader 2: As we light our second Advent candle, we think of preparing our hearts to receive the Christ child. We wait for God to teach us, to give us courage, and to bring justice to all the problems of our world. Let us prepare for Advent by finding a quiet place to wait.

Reader 3: Let us pray. We thank you, God, for your promise that you will come. Help us to learn patience through our waiting, so that we will be ready to greet you when you arrive. Amen.

THIRD SUNDAY IN ADVENT

Witness
John 1:6–8

Reader 1: "There was a man sent from God, whose name was John. He came as a witness to testify to the light, so that all might believe through him. He himself was not the light, but he came to testify to the light."

Reader 2: We light our third Advent candle to remind us that we need to tell others about Jesus. We need to share how God has touched, and continues to touch, our lives.

Reader 3: Let us pray. Dear God, sometimes we hide from your Word because we know that if we listen, we will have to share what we hear with strangers. And this scares us. Give us the courage to hold your light up so that others may see. Amen.

FOURTH SUNDAY IN ADVENT

Wonder
John 1:14

Reader 1: "And the Word became flesh and lived among us, and we have seen the glory, the glory of a parent's only child, full of grace and truth."

Reader 2: We light our fourth Advent candle today, and celebrate that God's mystery is about to be revealed. We express our wonder that God would choose to become one of us.

Reader 3: Let us pray. Dear Jesus, we have anticipated your birth with much expectation. We have been waiting for you to come for so long, and now our grief will be changed to joy! We give you thanks and sing in celebration. Amen.

Saint Andrew's Day

November 30

Andrew was Jesus' first disciple (John 1:35–42). Advent begins on the Sunday closest to Saint Andrew's Day.

Prayer for Saint Andrew's Day

Emmanuel, God with us, is it a lack of courage that keeps us from packing up our things and traveling with you? Is our vision clouded over? It is time to see you clearly, time to decide if we are going to follow your path, time to walk in your light. It is high time to be disciplined and cease doing what dissipates our energies, drains our dreams, and lessens our love. It is time to become fully alive; time to walk even though we stumble, endure detours as we roll along, and continue to run as we become tired. O God, like your first disciple, Andrew, help us to begin by simply traveling with you down your path.

Rosa Parks and World AIDS Day

December 1

On this day in 1955, Rosa Parks refused to move to the back of the bus and give up her seat to a white person. Her arrest was the spark that set the Montgomery bus boycott in motion.

Also on this day all those who have died or are living with AIDS and HIV, as well as their caregivers, are remembered as the search for a cure continues.

Prayer for Rosa Parks

God who sits, we have waited so long for your birth. We yearn to shed the night that threatens to overshadow us. We long with people of all generations to be sheltered in your presence. Today we remember Rosa Parks, who in 1955 gave birth to a movement for human rights by refusing to move to the back of the bus. Like her, we desire to be people of vision and strength, that we may know when to sit down and refuse to be moved by the immoral persuasion of racism, and that we may know when to stand up and be heard in the heroic fight against AIDS. O Light of the world, give us the vision to see that your warmth is needed, as well as your strength to carry it to those who are struggling to fend off the hollowing cold of despair. Amen.

Prayer for AIDS Day

God of Compassion, help us see what is going on around us and inside us. Help us focus today on the presence of AIDS in the world. Guide us in being sensitive to the needs of those who are afflicted—their families, partners, and caregivers. Let us remember those who are HIV-positive and struggling not to give up. Help them see each day as a new beginning, a new chance to grow closer to you. Help us not to fade like the sunset in a friend's eyes when times become difficult. Instead, let us watch for Christ's presence and for opportunities where we can be bearers of Christ's compassion. Let us be mindful that if we do not show our concern, Christ's love may not be felt. Help us realize that today is not a dress rehearsal for something that is coming. This is it! Amen.

I Didn't Worry about AIDS

Reader 1: In the 1970s, when "slims disease" started killing heterosexual women and men in Africa, I didn't pay much attention, because I didn't plan to travel to Africa.

Reader 2: In the 1980s, when a mysterious disease began killing gay men in the United States, I didn't worry about the lack of media coverage, because I figured it was a gay thing—and besides, *they* were always picking up exotic diseases.

Reader 1: When AIDS began infecting drug addicts who shared needles, I didn't worry about the lack of medical knowledge or the slowness of research on AIDS, because I didn't use drugs (at least not the kind that come through needles).

Reader 2: When heroin-addicted mothers began passing on the disease to their unborn children and hospital wards began filling up with these tiny creatures, my heart went out to them in their horrible suffering. But the government's slowness in responding to this situation didn't bother me, because I realized it took time to develop new medicines.

Reader 1: When surgical patients and people on kidney dialysis machines contracted AIDS through contaminated blood, I didn't worry about blood banks' refusal to improve their screening procedures, because I'd never had a blood transfusion and I didn't plan to have any surgery.

Reader 2: When college students and prostitutes began spreading the disease through heterosexual contact, I didn't worry about the government's refusal to talk about condoms and safe sex, because I didn't associate with college students or prostitutes.

Reader 1: When towns began to bar children with AIDS from school and force their families to leave town, I didn't pay much attention, because small towns are always picking on people who are different.

Reader 2: When AIDS was thought to have been transmitted from a dentist to his patient, I stopped going to dentists.

Reader 1: When seat cover dispensers appeared in the bathrooms at work, I stopped using the facilities.

Reader 2: When someone in church died of AIDS, I stopped going to church, because who knew where that person had been!

Reader 1: Each year as the dormant time for the virus increased—going from five, to seven, and then to ten years—I stopped becoming intimate with people. Who was safe? Although I may trust you, I'm not at all sure that I trust the people you were with a decade ago.

Reader 2: So now I stay home. I quit my job and began my own business on the Internet. I'm not seeing anyone, but if you write me, I promise to write a long letter in reply.

Reader 1: If we had known in the beginning what was going to happen, would we have done anything differently?

Reader 2: Now that we do know, is there anything we can do to catch up? Are there other problems just beginning to appear in our community to which we should pay attention?

Reader 1: Dear God, help us see clearly what is going on around us. Help us stand up and do what needs to be done now.

Reader 2:   Help us do the right thing—not the prudent thing, the wise thing, or even the nice thing—but the right thing. No matter what it costs us in public prestige. Amen.

Four Women Killed in El Salvador

December 2

On this day in 1980, after a number of years of following Christ's command to help the poor in El Salvador find food, clothing, and shelter, four American religious women—three nuns and a lay worker—were murdered by the Salvadoran military because what they were doing was regarded as subversive. Although they are not the only Christians to die in Central America for helping the poor, their deaths offer us a time to remember all who have died for following the gospel's call to care.

Liturgy of the Martyrs

This service is offered in memory of the deaths of Maura Clarke, Jean Donovan, Ita Ford, and Dorothy Kazel, Archbishop Oscar Romero, and the fifty thousand murdered and disappeared of El Salvador. The unrest in Central America is not over.

A period of silence is observed.

One: "Very truly, I tell you, unless a grain of wheat falls into the earth and dies, it remains just a single grain; but if it dies, it bears much fruit. Those who love their life lose it, and those who hate their life in this world will keep it for eternal life. Whoever serves me must follow me, and where I am, there will my servant be also. Whoever serves me, God will honor" (John 12:24–27).

One: Today as we begin to celebrate Advent, the coming of Christ into the world, let us also celebrate those who take Christ to others. The harvest is plentiful. The laborers are few. Come with me into the fields!

One: Our arms will grow weary, our shoes will wear thin, but we will follow our God throughout the world.

One: Today we remember those who have died while bearing the message of Christ in El Salvador, particularly the four church-women who were assassinated on December 2, 1980—Sister Maura Clarke, Jean Donovan, Sister Ita Ford, and Sister Dorothy Kazel. They went to a war-torn country to bring hope to the people of that land.

Many: These women did not go for their own glory, but for God's. They heard of the need, and their hearts were moved. And although they knew that they might be killed, as others had been killed before them, they still went. They felt they could do no less.

A READING

"Now my soul is troubled. And what should I say, 'God, save me from this hour'? No, it is for this reason that I have come to this hour" (John 12:27).

One: They worked and lived with the poor, doing what they could to relieve the misery and terror of daily life. While on a brief vacation back home in the United States, Jean had a premonition that if she returned to El Salvador, she would die there. But she felt she had to return. She was met at the airport by her three coworkers. On the way from the airport to the place where they were staying, soldiers of the government of El Salvador stopped them, raped them, tortured them, shot them, and buried them by the side of the road.

Christ hears the cry of the poor!

Many: Blessed be God!

One: Every crushed spirit God will lift up!

Many: Every fear God will shelter in caring arms!

One: Jesus will be a ransom for their lives! We proclaim the greatness of Christ. God's praise is ever on our lips!

Many: Every face brightens in God's light, for Jesus hears the cry of the poor!

One: We know that those who die in Christ's name do not die in vain. They go before us to prepare a place. But they are also with us, helping us to hear the depth of Christ's challenging word, daring us to enflesh God's Word with our lives, and showing us through the sacrifices of their lives how to hang on to hope when the world around us becomes a hell.

Many: What other thanks can we offer to God for our lives than to go to those whose hearts are broken and whose lives are heavy and offer them the faith that we bear in Christ's name?

One: May our hearts be firm so that we may stand before God, steadfast and unashamed, when Jesus Christ comes with all those who are God's own. Jean Donovan, you who left behind a comfortable life, a caring family, and a man who loved you, in order to share the life of poverty in El Salvador, are you here?

Many: (with uplifted arms) *Presente!*

One: Sisters Maura Clarke, Ita Ford, and Dorothy Kazel, you who first committed your lives to Christ with vows of poverty, chastity, and obedience, and (as if that weren't enough) then volunteered to risk your lives in El Salvador in hopes of healing the broken bodies and tattered lives of the powerless who faced death every day, are you here?

Many: *Presente!*

One: Archbishop Romero of El Salvador, who supported the status quo until you felt the gospel's call to witness and who stood up and preached God's love and reconciliation to all sides until you were cut down by bullets, and Bishop Gerardi of Guatemala, are you here?

Many: *Presente!*

One: You, the tortured bodies of the dead and disappeared of El Salvador, who were dragged away from your families in the middle of the night by death squads from the right and from the left, and who were mutilated and dismembered by those who value power over love, revenge over compassion, and money over God, are you here?

Many: *Presente!*

One: You, who live in powerful nations whose governments support the use of force for whatever reasons, whose international policies are made by business concerns instead of concern for human rights, and who seek not to build up but to tear down, are you here?

Many: *Presente!*

One: We are called to fight injustice and to seek righteousness in all lands; and if we do not, then the very stones of the ground will shout with martyrs' blood.

Many: There is no neutral ground in this struggle for life. If we promote justice, we must also be willing to accept the consequences. Following Christ is not easy or cheap.

One: Will you now work and pray, live and perhaps die, so that the love and healing power of Christ may touch the hearts of all who hate and seek to destroy?

Many: We will!

One: Will you offer comfort and sanctuary to all who are persecuted and driven from their homes and native lands?

Many: We will!

One: Will you value your own life so much that you are willing to risk it by combating the forces of evil wherever you hear of them? Are you willing to suffer the shame and confusion of being rejected by your own people for acting as Christians throughout history have acted?

Many: We are!

One: Then let us speak out against unjust laws. Let us object to murder and torture, to rape and terror. And let us invite others to do so.

All: We believe in God's presence in history. The world is not a roll of the dice. History does not repeat itself in endless cycles. Jesus' love lives among us; through the actions we take, this love can transform the world. Beyond the wounding of our bodies is the healing of our souls. The voices of the oppressed have been heard, and the powers of death are no more.

One: May Almighty God bless us: God who created us, Jesus who saves us, and the Spirit who sets us free. Amen.

PRAYER FOR THE MARTYRS

Peasant God, God of the poor, who feels all our pain, we remember today Maura Clarke, Jean Donovan, Ita Ford, and Dorothy Kazel, who went to war-torn El Salvador to bring hope to the displaced people of that country by bringing food, clothing, medicine, and shelter, and who were killed for their efforts in 1980. We thank you for their witness and pray that we may be strengthened enough to follow in their footsteps. In the name of the God who created us, Jesus who saves us, and the Spirit who challenges us to set others free, let us stand up with these women and declare ourselves "Presente!" Amen.

Feast of Saint Nicholas

December 6

Saint Nicholas was the Bishop of Myra in fourth-century Asia Minor. A number of traditions about him have developed over the years in a variety of countries. In one tradition, Nicholas secretly provided gold so that three girls could get married instead of being sold into slavery. In some countries, men dress up in white robes and give small presents to children, after encouraging them to be good. The name "Santa Claus" comes from the Dutch word for Saint Nicholas, "Sinterklaas." From Nicholas we also get the term "Father Christmas."

Litany: Images of Jesus

John 1:6–8, 19–28

One: John the Baptist said, "I baptize with water, but one who is coming will baptize you with the Spirit."

Many: But who is coming? People back then had many expectations for the Promised One, and today people have many expectations of the child born on Christmas.

One: When we look at Jesus, what do we expect to see in his face? Do we see his tiredness and worry, especially above the eyebrows?

Many: We know that Jesus lived as we do and was often worn down by the demands of daily life.

One: Do we see his anger and sadness over the difficulty people have in getting along with each other? Do we see his eyes inviting us to share in all the work that still needs to be done?

Many: We often feel that the gifts Jesus has given us don't amount to much. Many of us who have skills do not use them, and the world desperately needs all that we have.

One: Can we see the strong lines, the swirls of color on his face, and the flashes of light in his eyes? Do we see the shadows moving across his face?

Many: We know that Jesus enters our lives with broad motions that are unmistakable. He is dynamic and alive! He comes, and we are changed forever! Jesus is also with us in times when we are unsure and don't know what is going on.

One: Do we see Jesus waiting to walk alongside us?

Many: If so, then we see clearly and we have hope for the future.

One: The One who comes is coming for those who want help.

Jesus, in spite of all we've seen, we still have faith in your love. We know that you understand what this world is like. We can see the worry in your face, the look of seeing so much that needs to be done. Yet you never gave up hope; you were always sure that your coming would begin a new age of living. You knew that your gifts in us would enable us to continue your work, if we but took the time to sow and then harvest your seeds.

Sometimes we don't think we can do much because we lack possessions or deep spiritual wisdom. We often despair of making any difference in this world in the face of so much need. Give us the strength, this season, to expect great things of ourselves and of one another. Help us prepare. Help us give from our hearts of faith. Help us remember that long ago, in a tiny corner of an insignificant country, a child was born to parents of no importance, a child who would say, "Follow me and you will work miracles." And miracles are what we are called to do, with the help of a few seeds of faith. May this be so in our lives.

Immaculate Conception of Mary

December 8

This day honors the Roman Catholic belief that Mary, the mother of Jesus, was born sinless from the moment of her conception. It offers Protestants the opportunity to focus on Mary's willingness to receive the Good News and to let her life be changed because of it.

Prayer for the Immaculate Conception of Mary

Heavenly One, often we do not understand why you would want to be born into this world, why you said what you did, or even what you want us to do. But like Mary, who pondered it all in her heart and who provides a powerful example of how we can take you into our lives, we hold onto our questions. Help us live as though we understood your answers.

Our Lady of Guadalupe

December 12

In Mexico, devout people believe that the Virgin of Guadalupe was a reappearance of Mary, the mother of Jesus. She is also thought to have appeared to Bernadette at Lourdes, France, and to the three children at Fatima, Portugal. On this day, she appeared to Juan Diego and said she wanted a church built at that place to show her love, compassion, help, and protection for the people.

Prayer for Our Lady of Guadalupe

O God, help us listen to those who say they have seen visions, especially visions of you. It's not so much that we distrust what they are saying, but we are afraid of what they will do. And we are afraid of what they will want us to do. Help us listen to those who have experienced a transformation, and to be open to our own visions. And when we do see inexplicable things, may we have the patience to overcome the doubts of those who don't understand. Amen.

Saint Lucia's Day

December 13

On this day, people celebrate the life and death of a young girl who was killed by a Roman emperor for being a Christian. In Sweden the oldest daughter of the family, wearing a crown of lighted candles and a white robe, wakes up early and serves the members of her family a breakfast.

Prayer for Saint Lucia's Day

God of the catacombs, we view the death of this young Christian girl at the hands of the Romans as a tragedy, more so than if her parents had been killed. Yet we baptize and confirm our young in their faith, and we have to expect that they will want to witness to this. Help us listen to their excitement about their newfound faith with respect, even if the boldness of their proclamations makes us flinch. And help us to stand by them if they should suffer persecution. Amen.

Las Posadas

December 16

In Hispanic cultures, the nine days before Christmas see the reenactment of Joseph and Mary seeking lodging in Bethlehem and being turned away.

Prayer for *Las Posadas*

God of the road, we try to do what is right and follow the rules, but we aren't always successful. Sometimes we become like Mary and Joseph, hungry and tired from our travels, ending up where we don't want to be. Help us to believe that if we continue to try hard and make do with what comes our way, all will work out eventually. May we welcome the stranger and the needy when they come uninvited into our own lives. Amen.

Winter Solstice

December 22

The winter solstice in the Northern Hemisphere reminds us of our ancestors and how they dealt with the shorter days and longer nights, the solitude they felt when the sun rode low on the horizon and when the extended cold became a factor in their survival. This time of year is a time of returning to nature and carrying out rituals and celebrations that reconnect us with nature.

Prayer for the Winter Solstice

O God, the movement of our land to its greatest distance from the sun ends today. Now begins its turn back toward warmth and light, toward the end of winter and the beginning of spring. This time can also mark our turn from those plans of ours that lead nowhere toward a path that leads us closer to God. On this longest night, may we feel your presence and find dreams in the night sky to guide us home. Amen.

Hanukkah

Hanukkah, the Feast of Lights, is celebrated in December on the twenty-fifth day of the Hebrew month of *Kislev*. When the Syrian king Antiochus ruled Palestine, he attempted to force the Jewish people to worship Greek gods. In the process, he defiled the holy Temple in Jerusalem by burning incense to an idol on the altar of God. A rebellion led by Judas Maccabee in 167 B.C.E. drove the Syrians from Jerusalem. According to one story, when the Jews went to light the Temple's holy light, the Ner Tamid, they found that they only had enough oil for one day. Yet this oil lasted for eight days until additional holy oil could be found. Today Hanukkah is an eight-day celebration of the Maccabean victory, and a new candle is lit each day in remembrance of the miracle of the oil.

A Hanukkah Service for Christians

Each night the candles for the day are allowed to burn down and are replaced by new candles each subsequent night. As the candles are placed in the menorah, the focus of each previous night can be remembered. This service has been adapted for use by Christians, drawing guidance from the traditional Jewish service. Each night, the appropriate number of candles are placed in the menorah, starting from the right. The first two blessings are chanted. The day's candles are lit, and a prayer for that day's thankfulness is given. The service ends with the rededication prayer.

FIRST NIGHT OF HANUKKAH: GOD'S RESCUE

On the first night, a candle is placed in the holder on the far right of the menorah. The two blessings are chanted:

One: Blessed are you, Almighty God, Ruler of the universe. You hallow us with your *Mitzvot,* and command us to kindle the Hanukkah lights.

Many: Blessed are you, Almighty God. You saved the people of faith in generations past.

The first candle is lit, and thanks given, along the lines of:

One: (prayer of thankfulness) We thank you, God, for the devotion of those who fought for the faith, and for the renewal of your presence in the midst of our community. We thank you that we have been able to gather here tonight and worship you.

Many: (rededication prayer) We light this candle and rededicate our lives to God.

SECOND NIGHT OF HANUKKAH: THE GIFT OF LIGHT

One: Though all sometimes seems hopeless and dismal around us, we know that you have come to save your people in the past and will continue to do so in the future. We thank you for the communal spirit of this night, the gift of this light, and we rededicate ourselves to making sure that it does not go out. With your light as our guide, we are heartened in our struggles.

THIRD NIGHT OF HANUKKAH: REMINDERS OF GOD

One: We give you thanks for the reminders of your salvation: for the match that lights the wick, for the candles that shine with brightness, and for the flame that burns in this night and within our hearts.

FOURTH NIGHT OF HANUKKAH: THE FIGHT FOR FREEDOM

One: We give you thanks for the will to struggle for freedom, for the freedom to worship as we choose, for the freedom to be ourselves, and for the victory of the righteous over all those who would repress these freedoms and force their will upon the weak.

FIFTH NIGHT OF HANUKKAH: ENDURANCE

One: We give you thanks for those throughout the centuries who have endured and held on to their faith through self-sacrifice and persecution, even unto death. Their witness encourages us to persevere. Be with us when times are hard and we think of giving up hope and letting your light go out.

SIXTH NIGHT OF HANUKKAH: THE LIGHT OF SCRIPTURE

One: We give you thanks for the light of the Scriptures that guide us in our daily lives, asking that we may be considered worthy to carry this light into the world. Illuminate our minds and open our hearts.

SEVENTH NIGHT OF HANUKKAH: THE LIGHT OF WITNESS

One: We give you thanks for these Hanukkah lights. May they shine in our lives and in our homes throughout the coming year. May we be as brave as the Maccabees in standing up and protecting your gift of faith whenever this freedom is threatened.

EIGHTH NIGHT OF HANUKKAH: ONLY GOD'S LIGHT

One: Dear God, our final request is that you will always be the only light for us and our families. We acknowledge that it is only by your spirit that we endure and are able to combat injustice, hatred, and oppression. We pray for peace in the hearts of all people. May we never forget what you have done for us. May these Hanukkah lights shine before our eyes forever.

Christmas Eve

December 24

A Prayer for Christmas Eve

Reader 1:	In the darkness of Mary's womb, the holy child grew. In the shadows of the world's pain, there comes forth a blessed light.
Reader 2:	We light the Christ candle to remind us that Jesus, the child of radiant light, is the light of the world.
Reader 3:	Let us pray. Dear God, this is a night of joy! Make your light so shine in us that all who live near us will find new hope and join us in praising your holy name! Amen.

A Christmas Putz Story

A putz is a large-scale crèche, with scenes for each part of the Christmas story. This story is intended for five readers: a narrator, two men or boys and two women or girls.

Narrator:	This is a Christmas story. God sent the angel Gabriel to a woman minding her own business. She was engaged to be married to a man named Joseph. Gabriel appeared and said:
Male Reader 1:	Congratulations, Mary! God has an offer for you!
Narrator:	Confused by this unusual appearance and the personal notice from God, Mary tried to figure out what the angel's angle was.
Male Reader 1:	Don't be frightened, Mary, for God is going to bless you. Very soon now you will become pregnant and

have a baby boy. Joseph will not be the father, and yet he will be, for although he will have nothing to do with you becoming pregnant, the baby will be from Joseph's tree of Jesse. You are to name him "Jesus." He will be great and will be called the Child of God, the chosen One. He will reign over Israel forever and his reign will never end!

Narrator: Mary—full of faith yet not completely sure that she was really being asked to believe the unbelievable or completely clear about how it was going to happen—replied:

Female Reader 1: I am God's servant, and I am willing to do whatever God asks. If what you've said comes from God, may everything somehow come true.

Narrator: Shortly Mary realized that she was pregnant and that what the angel had told her was really true and not some strange dream. Joseph, aware of Mary's changing shape, decided to break the engagement in a way that would not publicly disgrace either Mary or himself. As he was thinking about how to accomplish this tricky maneuver, an angel appeared to him in a dream and said:

Female Reader 2: Joseph, don't be wary about making Mary your wife. She will give birth to a son and you will name him Jesus, because he will save his people from sin.

Narrator: When Joseph awoke, being full of faith himself, he did what the angel told him and married Mary (Matt. 1:18–25).

Then Augustus, the Roman emperor, said that everyone had to register for the census and they had to do so in the cities in which their ancestors were born. Because Joseph was a descendant of David, he had to travel to Bethlehem with a very pregnant Mary, who rode the long and hard miles on the hard, bony back of a donkey. As they reached Bethlehem, the time came for the baby to be born. She gave birth to her first son, wrapped him in a few strips of cloth, and laid him on a pile of hay arranged nicely in a feeding trough. The baby was born in a barn because Joseph and Mary were poor and couldn't afford to rent a room for the night.

An angel appeared to some tired, dirty shepherds who were tending their sheep and scared the life out of them. Eventually the angel calmed them down, saying:

Male Reader 2:   Don't be afraid! I am here with good news for you and for everyone. A baby has been born in Bethlehem tonight. And as proof, you can find the Messiah lying in a feeding trough in a barn.

Narrator: As the shepherds were laughing about the incongruity of this (and the funny sound of the word "incongruity"), suddenly this angel was joined by a great bunch of other angels, all singing:

All Four Readers: Glory to God in the highest heaven, and peace on earth to all who believe!

Narrator: This got the shepherds' attention. When the angels were gone, the shepherds—now no longer laughing, definitely no longer tired, and trying really hard to believe that this was actually happening—hurried off to the village. They poked their heads into various sheds until they found a couple that looked like Mary and Joseph and saw a baby that simply glowed. The shepherds edged their way inside and told those gathered what the angel had said about Jesus, and all who were there were sorely amazed (Luke 2:1–20).

About the same time, some astrologers from Persia arrived in Jerusalem and were asking around on the streets:

Female Reader 1: Where is the newborn king of the Jews? We saw his star from afar, way off in our country, and have come to honor him.

Narrator: King Herod heard the rumors and arranged a private meeting with these astronomers. He asked them the

	exact time they first saw the star. He did this so that he could have his staff astronomers figure out where the baby was and get there first. But he told the travelers:
Male Reader 1:	Go and search for the child. When you find him, come back here and tell me, so that I can go and worship him, too!
Narrator:	After the interrogation by Herod was over, the astronomers started out again. And there was the star, waiting for them over Bethlehem. Now the son of Mary was beautiful to behold (at least for a newborn), and when the Persians beheld Jesus, they got down on their knees. Then they took gold and silver from their bags, as well as myrrh and frankincense—all strange gifts for a baby shower but still very much appreci- ated—and laid them at the feet of Jesus. Then they fell down and prayed portentously in a strange tongue, which Mary and Joseph did not recognize. When morning came, the astronomers left. But before they saddled up, they said mysteriously:
Female Reader 2:	The child is but a day old, yet we have seen the light of our God in his eyes and the smile of our God on his mouth. We bid you to take care of him and to listen to him when he grows up and has something to say.
Narrator:	And so saying wisely, they smoothly mounted their camels and slid off into the shimmering desert and toward the rising, shining sun, returning home by another route of trade. Another angel, one in God's apparently endless line of angels, appeared to Joseph in a second dream, saying:
Male Reader 2:	Get up and run away as fast as you can to Egypt with the baby and his mother. Stay there until King Herod dies, for he wants to kill the child.
Narrator:	So Joseph and Mary took baby Jesus and did as the angel had instructed, heading for the border (Matt. 2:1–15).

Midnight Service of Light and Shadows

Allowance may need to be made in this service for those with mobility or vision limitations. Large-print bulletins may help all worshipers in the dim light.

Once everyone is seated, at 11:00 P.M., turn the lights off and allow a few minutes for quiet to settle over the congregation. Only the nave candles are lit. There is no prelude. The choir, musicians, and readers are in the balcony or at the back of the sanctuary if there is no balcony.

INTROIT
A light rhythm begins on one drum. One by one, the other drums and percussion instruments join in:

First drum (mid-range): *1   a2   a3   a4a&a*
Second drum (higher): *1   2a&a3   4a&a*
Third drum (lower): *1   &a2   &a3   (4)*
Bongos: *1a &a2a&a3a&a4a&a*

Handbells begin to ring randomly. The choir members softly sing "O Come, O Come, Emmanuel." After the choir has a good start, the narrator begins the first reading.

READING 1: DARKNESS
A long time ago, people lived in gloom, in lands covered with fears and shadows of empty nights. Every day people worried that they might not survive the night, believing for the most part that tomorrow would be no better. Every day was a struggle to find enough food. Every day people died after brief lives cut short by famine, disease, and war. Marauding nations overran other nations, taking entire populations into exile, slavery, and death. Chaos reigned. The law of the land was to do whatever it took to survive. With desperation barely held at bay, people thought little about the future.

Yet in this time of deep gloom and trouble, God spoke to those who dared dream of something better. In the respite of the night, when people rested from their labors, some quietly searched the stars for signs of hope. To them God brought balm for their wounds. In the deepest time of the night, when even the moon was absent, there was a place still deeper, where God could be found. This was the land within the dark, the still place, the land on the other side of the city walls, walls that kept people from seeing beyond their daily lives and dreaming of what might be.

From night to night, God's voice spoke to those who waited in silent worship. In the whispers of God people heard the reassurances they needed: "Don't give up. I am with you." From darkness to deeper darkness, God's song moved in them with the rhythms of life. Those who prayed through the watches of the night found their faith in the unending depths of God's mystery. Those who would not give up hope found strength to continue. As heralds from a time long ago, they lived as witnesses to the eternal.

PROCESSION

There is a pause as everyone in the balcony comes downstairs to the back of the sanctuary. Then drums and bells resume their cadence. The narrator begins the second reading, during which the four Advent candles are processed in, lit, with the unlit Christ candle in the middle. The procession stops in the middle aisle by the front pews, with those holding the Advent candles facing in toward the Christ candle.

READING 2: PROMISE

To those who did not give up hope, to those trying to discern the treasures of darkness, Isaiah spoke of a child who would be born:

> The people who walked in darkness have seen a great light; those who lived in a land of deep shadows—on them has light shined. You have multiplied the nation, you have increased its joy; the people rejoice before you as with joy at the harvest, as victors rejoice when dividing the spoil. For the yoke of their burden, and the bar across their shoulders, the rod of their oppressor, you have broken as on the day of Midian.
>
> For all the boots of the tramping warriors and all the garments rolled in blood shall be burned as fuel for the fire. For a child has been born to us, to us an heir is given; authority rests upon the shoulders of that one whose name will be called Wonderful Counselor, Mighty

God, Everlasting Father and Mother, Prince of Peace. That one's authority shall grow continually, and there shall be endless peace for the throne of David and David's kingdom, to establish it and to uphold it with justice and with righteousness from this time onward and forevermore (based on Isa. 9:2–7).

And for seven hundred years, with this promise clutched firmly to their chests, the people who had waited so long for hope, began to hope.
The choir sings alone the first verse of "O Come, O Come, Emmanuel"; the congregation joins in starting with the second verse. During the hymn, the choir processes in the semidarkness along the outside aisles to the choir loft.

CALL TO WORSHIP

Reader 1: Birthday child and gift for the ages, we see so much hardness surrounding us that it is easy to give up hope, easy to begin to despair of life.

Many: Help us hang on to the promise of Isaiah whenever day-to-day life wears us down.

Reader 1: Let us look for glimmers of the dawn through the gloom, and walk toward the light.

Many: Help us believe that Jesus really was born and will be born again this year in our lives!
Pause.

Reader 2: In anticipation we gather . . .

Many: With expectations we wait . . .

Reader 2: We gather to hear the good news . . .

Many: We wait for the One long promised . . .

Reader 2: Let our worship begin!

CANDLE LIGHTING

As the following is read, the Christ candle is lit by the four Advent candles, and all five candles are processed the rest of the way in and placed on the communion table or altar.

Reader 1: In the darkness of Mary's womb, the holy child grew. In the shadows of the world's pain, there has come forth a blessed light.

Reader 2: We light the Christ candle to remind us that Jesus, the child of radiant light, is the Light of the world.

Reader 1: Let us pray. Dear God, this is a night of joy! Make your light so shine in us that all who live near us will find new hope and join us in praising your holy name!

During the singing of "O Little Town of Bethlehem," the candles on the pillars and/or in the windows of the sanctuary are lit.

READING 3: THE BIRTH

In those days, a decree went out from Emperor Augustus that all the world should be registered. This was the first registration and was taken while Quirinius was governor of Syria. All went to their own towns to be registered. Joseph also went from the town of Nazareth in Galilee to Judea, to the city of David called Bethlehem, because he was descended from the house and family of David. He went to be registered with Mary, to whom he was engaged and who was expecting a child. While they were there, the time came for her to deliver her child. She gave birth to her first-born son, wrapped him in bands of cloth, and laid him in a manger, because there was no place for them in the inn.

In that region, there were shepherds living in the fields, keeping watch over their flock by night. Then an angel of God stood before them, and the glory of God shone around them, and they were terrified. But the angel said to them, "Do not be afraid; for see—I am bringing you good news of great joy for all people: to you is born this day in the city of David a savior, who is the Messiah. This will be a sign for you: you will find a baby wrapped in bands of cloth and lying in a manger." And suddenly there was with the angel a multitude of the heavenly host, praising God and saying, "Glory to God in the highest heaven, and on earth peace among those with whom God is pleased!" (based on Luke 2:1–14).

As the singing of "Away in a Manger" commences, the lights begin to come up slowly.

READING 4: WITNESSES

When the angels had left them and gone into heaven, the shepherds said to one another, "Let us go to Bethlehem and see this thing that has taken place, which God has made known to us." So they went with haste and found Mary and Joseph, and the baby lying in the manger. When they saw this, they made known what had been told them about this child; and all who heard it were amazed at what the shepherds told them. But Mary treasured all these words and pondered them in her heart. The shepherds returned, glorifying and praising God for all they had heard and seen, as it had been told them (based on Luke 2:15–20).

When the Magi had heard the king, they set out; and there, ahead of them, went the star that they had seen at its rising, until it stopped over the place where the child was. When they saw that the star had stopped, they were overwhelmed with joy. On entering the house, they saw the child with Mary, his mother; and they knelt down and paid him homage. Then, opening their treasure chests, they offered the child gifts of gold, frankincense, and myrrh. And having been warned in a dream not to return to Herod, they left for their own country by another road (based on Matt. 2:9–12).

OFFERING
Before the offering, all join in the hymn "Hark the Herald Angels Sing," and Christmas prayers are offered. A soloist then sings "Ave Maria" or another suitable piece. The offering is followed by the singing of "It Came upon the Midnight Clear."

READING 5: MINISTRY
Luke 2–3
The shepherds and Magi who saw Jesus' birth returned to their homes and shared what they had seen. And the light grew stronger as family shared with family, friends shared with friends, and word began to spread that maybe this was the One foretold by Isaiah so long ago.

For the next thirty years, Jesus grew in wisdom and stature. John the Baptist began to preach his message of repentance and to baptize people in the desert. People flocked to him, and to them he said, "Wait a short while now. The one who was promised is about to come. I am nothing compared to him." And Jesus began his ministry. For three short years, the dreams nurtured in shadows merged with the light, and the mystery of God was seen in all its fullness.
All join in singing "O Come, All Ye Faithful."

Reading 6: Today

Two thousand years later, the dreams of darkness and the hopes of light still make up our lives. The dreams of darkness give us direction and sustain us when the light falters. The hopes of light bring us courage and break the never-ending night into pieces of memory and unending day into shadows of thoughts. No more is despair complete. No longer is hope something to be put off for the next generation. A new day has begun to dawn! Nights of prayer have replaced nights of despair—nights as sacred gates through which God waits for us!

Isaiah said, "Upon your walls, O Jerusalem, I have posted sentinels; all day and all night they shall never be silent. Go through, go through the gates, prepare the way for the people; build up, build up the highway, clear it of stones, lift up a banner over the peoples. The Almighty has proclaimed 'See, your salvation comes!'" (based on Isa. 62:6, 10–11).

Prayer

As this prayer is offered, the lights begin to come down and the choir members begin to light their candles from the Christ candle and gather at the front of the chancel. The Advent and Christ candles stay up front.

Now there is light to go with the darkness. Too much darkness, and people collapse from overburden. Too much light, and people wither and become barren as deserts. The light has come to join the darkness and fulfill its dreams. Together the two reveal the fullness of God. Starlight, candle lights, porch lights. In our world of dimly seen visions, Christ's light beckons us home.

As the choir members sing "Good Christian Friends Rejoice," they silently move to the outside aisles and surround the congregation. The lights come down the rest of the way, leaving only candlelight.

Do not hide from the short, gloomy days of December. Embrace them as a time to be cherished. Nurture the expectations of promise growing within you. Let shadows have a place in this mystery. Allow space for the unknown of God to move about.

Do not let this light shine only for this night. Let it shine down into your fears. Let your despair dissolve in this candlelight as the wax of the candle melts and nourishes the wick; let hope rise with the flame.

Do you see the darkness? Do you feel a presence? As the candlelight moves among us, shadows cast doubts upon our fears. Only when we let go of our self-serving ambitions will the darkness reveal its light, only then will God whisper in a quiet place, and only then will we hear with the heart of our dreams.

When we go outside tonight and on the nights to come, look up at the stars. Remember all those who have gone before us, who stood in the shadows looking up, and found hope in the stillness when more rational minds were saying there was no hope. Look up and believe that on this night, long ago, a baby was born who would be a savior for all! That on this night suddenly people had reason to hope again, and remembered how to laugh and sing and dance with joy! That on this night God came and stood among us as one of us! That on this night of all nights, we no longer need to fear death or principalities or things above or below the earth. For on this night, the light of the world is born! Amen.

RECESSIONAL
While singing "Silent Night," the choir lights the candles of the people at the end of the pews. These people pass the light down their pews toward the center aisle. The candles on the side of the pillars facing the back are lit now. The worship leaders and the acolytes go to the middle of the congregation and invite everyone to face them.

UNISON BENEDICTION
Reader 1: As light has come into the world for us, let us become light for the world.

All: Most gracious God, we give you all our thanks for the gift of the Christ child. May we be as birth mothers, helping Christ be born in the lives of those around us. As sentinels up on the city walls see the dawn gathering on the horizon, may we now see the dawning of God's reign in our hearts, and may we then carry this light everywhere we go in our world. Amen.

Reader 2: Go now with the light of God safely burning within your hearts. Amen.

The congregation extinguishes its candles at this point. Leaders and the choir keep their candles lit. The worship leaders and acolytes recess down the main aisle, and the choir moves up the outside aisles to the center aisle and then recesses single file to the back, with their candles still lit.

POSTLUDE

After the leaders and the choir members have fully recessed, the drums and bells pick up their music from the start of the service, playing softly. The only lights in the choir loft are the Advent and Christ candles. In the main part of the sanctuary, only the pillar candles (or the side aisle lights if there are no pillar candles) are providing light. An alternative would be for the choir to keep their candles lit at the back of the sanctuary while they softly sing, and the congregation is dismissed.

Feast of Stephen

December 26

The day after the birth of Jesus was chosen to honor Stephen as the first Christian martyr (Acts 6–7). The carol about good King Wenceslas going out on this date in a winter storm to bring food and firewood to poor people continues this witness. Wenceslas lived in the tenth century and helped spread Christianity throughout Bohemia.

Prayer for the Feast of Stephen

One who seeks to heal, it is so hard to risk our own comfort when speaking of you, to put ourselves into danger in order to help those who are in danger get out. Yet we know that if we do so, we will find a place like Stephen's, where fear and violence will not concern us. Surrounded by violence, we will feel only peace. O God, strengthen us to be bold in our witness. Amen.

Kwanzaa

December 26–January 1

Kwanzaa is an African American holiday developed in 1966 as a cultural celebration by Maulana Krenga, a professor of African American studies at California State University at Long Beach. It is a synthesis of African spiritualities that celebrate the values of collective work and cultural principles. The foundation of Kwanzaa rests upon the *nguzo saba,* the "seven principles of blackness." They are: *umoja* (unity), *kujichagulia* (self-determination), *ujima* (collective work and responsibility), *ujamaa* (cooperative economics), *nia* (purpose), *kuumba* (creativity), and *imani* (faith). One principle is celebrated each day from December 26 through January 1. People come together for daily ceremonies, often in the evenings, and discuss how to apply the principles to their lives. On the last day, everyone celebrates.

The preparations for the festival can be fairly simple. A straw mat *(mkeka)* is placed on a table. The mat stands for African American history and traditions. On the mat is a candle holder *(kinara)* for family members who have died, and seven candles *(mishumaa saba),* one candle for each of the seven principles. The center candle is black, for African American people. The three candles to one side are red, for the past and present struggles. The three candles on the other side are green, for future hopes. A basket of fruits and vegetables *(mazao)* is placed on the table and represents the harvest, ears of corn *(muhindi)* for the importance of children, and a cup *(kikombe cha umoja)* for unity.

The family gathers at the same time each day, usually before the evening meal. One person lights a candle and speaks about the day's principle. Then everyone else takes a turn saying why she or he thinks the principle is important. Family members who have died are remembered, and some of the water or juice in the cup is poured out into a bowl to honor them. The candle lighter drinks from the cup, raises it, and says *"Harambee!"* ("Let's all work together!") Everyone says *"Harambee!"* once on the first day and seven times at the end, once for each principle. The cup is passed, and everyone drinks from it. Then the names of African American leaders and heroes are called out, and everyone discusses why these people were important. After the meal, the family sings and listens to African music.

Other symbols that can be included in the festivities are the African American flag of Marcus Garvey (with its black, red, and green stripes), Kwanzaa cards, and the greeting *"Habari Gani"* ("What's new?"), with the answer being the principle of the day.

Rituals for the Seven Days of Kwanzaa

FIRST DAY: *UMOJA*—BEING JOINED TOGETHER

The candle lighter says something like "Today is the first day of Kwanzaa. I light the black candle that stands for unity; it means that we need to work together for peace in our families, our neighborhoods, cities, and nation." All present talk about the principle, remember family members who have died, drink from the cup, and shout *"Harambee!"*

SECOND DAY: *KUJICHAGULIA*—BEING YOURSELF

The black candle is lit, then one red candle. The discussion is about how important it is for African American people to decide for themselves what they will say and do and what they will be.

THIRD DAY: *UJIMA*—WORKING TOGETHER

The first two candles are lit, then the first green candle. Everyone discusses the need for working together to satisfy the community's need for food, clothing, housing, and jobs, and to address the problems of drugs and violence.

FOURTH DAY: *UJAMAA*—SHARING RESOURCES

The second red candle is lit, and a discussion follows about the need to share work and resources with one another, both at home and in business.

FIFTH DAY: *NIA*—HAVING GOALS

The second green candle is lit. We talk about how important it is to have goals for the future and also to be willing to help one another succeed.

SIXTH DAY: *KUUMBA*—CREATIVITY

The last red candle is lit. People talk about how they express their own creativity—whether it be in woodworking, storytelling, sewing, writing, painting, or singing—and how being creative is important in making our community a better and more beautiful place. Often families join together to celebrate at a community center on this night and hold a *Karamu* feast with a lot of African food, music, and dancing.

Before the feast begins, a *tamshi la tambiko* (a short speech offering thanks) is given, like the following:

We gather tonight to offer thanks for what we have:
the wisdom of our elders,
the promise in our youth,
and the leaders of our community.
We also give thanks for
this wonderful food,
and reminders of the greatness of our African culture.
We give thanks for our unity
as a community that continues to discover itself,
to grow, and in affirming who we are.

The unity cup is filled with water, held up in the direction of the four winds, and passed around to each person. Two gifts are given to each child. One is a book, and the other is a handmade gift representing Africa. At the end of the *Karamu* celebration, a farewell statement is given which speaks of hope for the new year.

Seventh Day: *Imani*—Having Faith

Imani begins right after *Kuumba* ends at midnight. The singing and dancing stop, and the last candle is lit. People talk about what they believe and of the need to believe—in themselves, in their neighborhoods, and in the continuing struggle for justice. They talk about the past year and the mistakes they made, about their goals for the new year and what they hope to accomplish. For the last time, the cup is poured and raised up. The leader says *"Harambee!"* and everyone shouts *"Harambee!"* back seven times.

Boxing Day

December 26

The tradition of Boxing Day dates back to the Middle Ages in Great Britain. On December 26, the church's poor box is opened and the money shared with the poor. A variation of this tradition involves people putting money in small boxes and giving them to those who have been of service to them in the past year.

Prayer for Boxing Day

On this day after Christmas, we remember those among us, O God, who have not had happy celebrations, who have not eaten more than they should, who have not opened mounds of presents, but who are instead cold and hungry and tired and alone. May we take a tithe of our gifts and today do something to help the poor. Even the remnants of a feast are still a banquet to those who weren't originally invited. Amen.

Feast of Saint John

December 27

This feast commemorates Saint John, apostle, evangelist, and Jesus' beloved disciple. The Gospel of John was probably written by him.

Prayer for Saint John

Sometimes we hide from your Word, God, because we know that if we listen, we will have to share what we hear with strangers. And this scares us. Sometimes we are amazed that you even chose to become one of us. Give us the courage to receive your Word into our lives in ways that move us deeper into ministry. Amen.

Holy Innocents Day

December 28

This day commemorates the infants who were killed by Herod as he tried to find and kill the baby Jesus.

Prayer for the Holy Innocents

God who is God, when we experience the shaking of what we have always thought to be solid, we are overwhelmed. When horrors happen, when the powerful brutalize the weak in order to keep what they have, we find it hard to believe that you are a God at all. When we find out about all the innocent children killed by Herod in an attempt to kill the baby

Jesus, we lose our bearings, and it seems as if there's nothing left to hold on to. Sometimes we have trouble believing that all things hold together in Christ, no matter what happens. O God, help us hold on to belief, even when it seems it is being torn down. Amen.

Watchnight

December 31

This is a midnight service that summarizes the past year. In recent centuries, the Moravians and early Methodists have celebrated it as a vigil service focusing on newness, the spiritual life, and covenants. In some churches, people write individual covenants with God on pieces of paper which then are collected. These are then mailed to them six months later so they can see how faithful they have been to their promises.

Prayer for Watchnight

O Quiet within voices, where are the voices that lead us to faith? Where are the voices that confront our lives when they become comfortable? If the voices come from too far away, do we distrust them? And if they come from too close by, do we discount them? To whom do we listen? Do we listen to anyone who speaks with conviction, or do we always have to be our own persons and go along our own path by ourselves? O God, help us be quiet. Help us listen for the voices that will speak to us tonight. Amen.

Liturgy of Covenanting, Watchnight

All stand.

One: Seek Jesus while he may be found. Call upon God while God is still near. Let those who take advantage of others forsake their harmful ways and the proud their thoughts. Let them return to Christ's way, and Christ will have mercy upon them. Let us pray together the prayer that Jesus taught.
        All pray the Prayer of Our Savior.

One: Blessed are those whose lives are selfless, who do the work of Christ with mercy and compassion. Blessed are those who seek Christ with all their hearts, and speak of God's presence wherever they go.

Many: May we be steadfast in keeping God's directions, for then we will not be ashamed when our deeds come to light.

One: The ways of God are hard, the door is narrow, the path uncertain, but they bring joy to the heart.

Many: The commandments of Christ are pure, enlightening the eyes. The fear of Christ directed us away from frivolous diversions.

One: More desired are they than money, even more than a fortune. By them, God's servants are warmed. In keeping them, there is grace.

Many: Lead us on the path of your commandments, O God, for in them we delight. Teach us your wisdom.

One: God spoke these words: "You shall have no other gods before me. You shall not worship anything or anyone but me. You shall not take my name in vain. Remember the Sabbath to keep it holy. Honor your parents. Do not kill. Do not commit adultery. Do not steal. Do not bear false witness against your neighbor, or desire anything that is your neighbor's." Jesus said, "A new commandment I give you, that you love one another as I have loved you. By this shall all people know that you are my disciples."

Many: We will meditate on God's rules and respect God's ways. We will not forget the words that God speaks.

One: As Jesus willingly gave up his life for others, may God give us the strength and grace to present our bodies as a living sacrifice for the needs of others, for this is our reasonable service.

Many: We put on the yoke of Christ, that Christ may guide us in all we do and say. Dear God, save us from conforming to the values of this world, and from thinking more highly of ourselves than we should.

One: Save us from thinking ourselves wise in our folly and from being overcome by the illusions of our own success. Enable us to heal hatred and anger with love and respect.

Many: Hear us and help us, we ask you.

One: When we have not kept you in our thoughts, when we have despised your mercy as weakness, when our hearts have been hard and unrepentant, when we have dishonored you by denying that we know you and denying that we have hope to offer others,

Many: Forgive us, we beg you.

One: O Lamb of God, who takes away the sins of the world,

Many: Send us your spirit!

One: Let us pray:

All: Yearning God, we remember the covenant you made with Abraham and Sarah—that you would be their God if they would be your people. You yearn to make the same covenant with us, with Jesus the Christ as the mediator of the new covenant. If you will be with us when we are afraid, despairing, and lost, we pledge to live no more for our own gain, but only for service to you. We take time now to renew our covenant with you.

One: I invite each of you to come forward and kneel when you are ready. Examine the past year to see where you have fallen short in faith or practice of your commitment. Then come, let go of this failure. Take communion when you are up front. Pick up a piece of writing paper and return to your seat. Write down how you want to renew your covenant with God over the coming year. The paper will be collected and mailed back to you in six months so that you can see how faithful you have been.

Music of covenanting is played. Collection of covenants follows.

BENEDICTION

One: A new year has begun. Go now and live your lives completely dedicated to Christ.

Many: We are a new covenant people. We will now live as such.

Naming and Circumcision of Jesus

January 1
In Hebrew tradition, a baby's dedication was done eight days after birth (Luke 2:21; Lev. 12:3).

Prayer for the Naming and Circumcision of Jesus

God of all names, the names given to us by our parents sometimes fit us and sometimes do not. Some of us grow into them or find nicknames that suit us better. We know that American Indians often found their names from visions they had, visions that brought them power and guidance. Today we remember the naming of Jesus and the covenant with you. Jesus' name means "God saves" or "Savior," and while this was certainly a major focus in his life, this name does not summarize all that he was or means to us. Let us mention some of those names now. We know that you call us by name. May we be proud of our names and proud of the heritage they represent. And may we allow you to call us by our inner name, the one waiting in your vision of our future. Amen.

Epiphany

January 6
This date celebrates the arrival of the Magi (the three kings).

Prayer for Epiphany

Little One, we stand as the Magi stood, gazing in awe at you, watching you beaming and shining in your warm blanket. Somehow we know that through you all our dreams will be fulfilled. Welcome. Amen.

4

~~

Season after Epiphany

The season after Epiphany lasts from four to nine Sundays, beginning on January 7 and ending on Ash Wednesday with the beginning of Lent. Although it is not an official season like the seasons of Advent and Lent, this period focuses on the manifestations of Jesus' divinity: the baptism of Jesus by John the Baptist, when the Spirit descended; the first miracle at Cana, when Jesus turned water into wine during a wedding celebration; and the transfiguration of Jesus on the mountain.

The season after Epiphany echoes the themes of Christmas and Epiphany. The liturgical color is green, except for the Sundays when the baptism and the transfiguration are remembered; then the color is white. This season is also a period for remembering that Jesus healed those who came to him, and called disciples to help him in his ministry.

The celebrations in January include the baptism of Jesus, Martin Luther King Jr. Sunday, the confession of Peter, and the conversion of Paul. In February, many churches celebrate Black History Month with a variety of historical, liturgical, and cultural events. Other celebrations in February include the presentation of Jesus in the Temple and the Feast of the Transfiguration.

The Baptism of Jesus

Sunday after January 6

If a covenant service was not used on New Year's Eve, the Sunday of Jesus' baptism is an appropriate time for the members of a congregation to renew their covenant with God.

Liturgics for the Baptism of Jesus

Isaiah 42:1–9

CALL TO WORSHIP

One: God predicts and then makes happen.

Many: God says, "I will send my servant, and my servant will not fail or be discouraged until justice has been established in the earth."

One: God sent Jesus to make the dream possible.

Many: Jesus sends us to make the dream come true.

PRAYER FOR THE BAPTISM OF JESUS

God, how hard it is for us to believe. Today we remember when John baptized Jesus in the river, when the Holy Spirit descended upon him in the form of a dove and when a voice from heaven was heard declaring this young man to be God's own. We find it hard to understand that all those present did not go home as believers and tell others. Why have we not heard of these later witnesses? Did those present not believe what they saw and heard? Did others not believe their testimony? By the end of this season after Epiphany, when we will have looked at the other special events that gave people clues into Jesus' divinity, will we believe any more deeply than those earlier witnesses did that Jesus really is who we have been looking for all these years?

UNISON PRAYER

Christmas is over now, God, yet we still savor memories of twinkling lights, Christmas carols, and special foods. We feel a hope that everything we've long desired is now possible. We have dreams of how life should be, and we don't want this to end. But how do we hang on to these feelings throughout the year? How do we personalize these dreams and make something happen in our lives? At the very least, we can commit ourselves to do what we feel comfortable doing. Much good has been done by people simply taking a moment to be kind, helpful, or considerate. We can also go further and probe the edges of where we begin to feel uncomfortable, and do a few things that scare us a little. You did not call us to wait and see what happens in the new year. Through Isaiah you said, "I have given you as a covenant to the people, a light to the nations." Help us go from here as partners in your covenant for all people; for through us, because of Jesus, your future comes to be. Amen.

Martin Luther King Jr. Sunday

Sunday nearest January 15

Martin Luther King Jr. Service

WORDS OF PREPARATION
"One day we shall win our freedom, but not only for ourselves. We shall so appeal to your heart and conscience that we shall win you in the process, and our victory will be a double victory." (Martin Luther King Jr.)

After a prelude, the choir and congregation join in the processional hymn, "Lift Every Voice and Sing," by James Weldon and John Rosamond Johnson.

CALL TO WORSHIP
One: Your love, Yahweh, reaches to heaven; your faithfulness to the skies.

Many: Your justice is like a mountain; your judgments like the deep. To all creation you give protection.

One: Your people find refuge in the shelter of your wings.

Many: They feast on the riches of your house; they drink from the stream of your delight.

One: You are the source of life, and in your light we see light.

Many: Continue your love to those who know you, doing justice to the upright in heart (based on Ps. 36:5–10).

A hymn is sung, followed by the reading of Isaiah 62:1–4 and the anthem "Precious Lord, Take My Hand," by Thomas A. Dorsey.

MEDITATION

A Reading for Martin

Reader 1: Dear brother, what have we done to you?

Reader 2: What have we done to your dream? Did we really know who you were?

Reader 1: Did we want to know?

Reader 2: Were you ready to be the hero for us?

Reader 1: Were we ready to heed your call for freedom and justice? Are we ready now?

Reader 2: You showed us how to be true to our faith by putting your own life on the line. You reminded us that we are here not to live long lives (although that has its place), but to carry the message of Jesus Christ to all people.

Reader 1: You allowed yourself to be beaten and imprisoned, spat upon and threatened, until they finally murdered you. But your voice has not been stilled.

Reader 2: Your words continue to challenge us, to irritate our reasonable plans, to move us into places that we aren't sure we want to go.

Reader 1: You were a pastor and a leader, a seeker and a teacher, a husband and a father. You held up the Constitution and the Bible and challenged us to see the connections.

Reader 2: So often you were a step ahead of us, and we struggled to catch up to the fullness of your vision. From civil rights for African Americans, you encouraged us to see everyone's rights; from economic segregation, you tried to move us to see that institutionalized poverty trapped even more people of all cultures. And in the midst of it all, you showed us that change is possible, but only if we were willing to take a chance and speak out for justice.

Reader 1: You saw deeper than most of us and realized that justice involved more than just changing laws. It involved changing hearts.

Reader 2: Many years have passed since the Montgomery bus boycott of 1955. Over the next thirteen years, you marched and went to jail to desegregate lunch counters and washrooms. Your march on Washington in 1963 expressed the soul of a generation and led to the passage of the Civil Rights Act and the Voting Rights Act.

Reader 1: Wherever people were beaten down, you were there to lift them up.

Reader 2: While some pushed only for black power and black rights, you spoke of the need to continue to uphold human power and human rights.

Reader 1: We find it hard to believe that more than thirty years have passed since your death. What have we done since then? We have lost your vision and betrayed your dream. The struggle is far from over. Each day a little more is chipped away from the gains for which you died.

Reader 2: If Martin were here today, would we be ready this time? And if he questioned our values and our bank accounts, how would we respond? What would Martin say of our support of governments for political and economic gains but not for gains in education and justice?

Reader 1: But we have not gathered here today just to remember Martin Luther King Jr. We are here to remember his words and to find ways to keep his dream alive. Let us resolve to walk with Martin in the dream and build a better future.

Both
Readers: The word was justice. It was spoken. So it shall be spoken. So it shall be done. Amen.

Unison Prayer

Compassionate God, we pray for justice because your people are suffering the effects of greed, power, and racism in this world. We pray for healing, that we may recover from the effects of violence and deprivation in our lives. We pray for your good news, that we may find hope to dream again about the future. And we pray for peace, that we may all find joy in sitting together as brothers and sisters under fig trees and not being afraid (Micah 4:4). Amen.

WORDS OF ASSURANCE

Yahweh, ever faithful, sends justice to those who have been denied it, healing to those who are broken, good news to those eager to hear, and peace to our hearts and minds so that we may trust one another again and bear one another's burdens.

The closing hymn is sung: "Keep the Dream Alive," by Robert Manuel.

BENEDICTION

May God grant us visions of truth, faith to witness in the midst of injustice, courage to endure, and the hope to carry us to the end. Go forth now as a people of justice. Amen.

Week of Prayer for Christian Unity

January 18–25

January 18 commemorates the confession of Saint Peter, and January 25 the conversion of Saint Paul. Because of the importance of Peter among Catholics and Paul among Protestants, the eight days encompassing these two dates is a time for ecumenical observances.

Confession of Saint Peter

January 18

Mark 8:27–35 records Peter's answer to Jesus' question, "Who do people say that I am?" Peter said that Jesus was the long-awaited Messiah. This was the first time that anyone had acknowledged this truth.

A Litany of Confession

> *Mark 8:27–35*

One: God is in the holy Temple. Let all the earth keep silence. The mighty God, the One we look to for our lives, speaks and calls the earth to come near, from the rising of the sun until its going down.

Many: We lift up our hands in this sanctuary and praise God. We stand up and thank our God forever and ever!
All who can stand should do so.

One: Dear Jesus, in spite of all our difficulties to fully believe, help us declare with Peter that you indeed are the Promised One, you indeed are the Messiah. Let us claim you as our Savior and go to worship on God's holy hill, for God alone is holy!

Many: But who will walk up the hill of God? Who will stand on top, in God's holy place?

One: Those who have clean hands and pure hearts, those who do not lift up their soul to what is false and do not speak for their own gain.

Many: If we say that we do not sin, we deceive ourselves and the truth is not in us.

One: If we confess our sins, God is faithful and just to forgive us our sins and to cleanse us from all unrighteousness. We have an advocate with God, Jesus Christ the righteous, and Christ is the atoning sacrifice for our sins.

Many: And not just for our sins, but also for the sins of the whole world.

One: Let us draw near in full assurance of faith, confess our sins, and present our supplications before God. Let us pray.
All who can kneel should do so.
Almighty God who lives in eternity, whose name is holy, who dwells in the high and holy places with those of humble spirits, give us the grace to bring you our broken and contrite hearts, which you, O God, do not despise. Hear us, gracious God.
We confess that we have not watched for your presence, waited for your guidance, or witnessed to your love in the midst of our doubts. We are quick to assume a privileged place and slow to welcome the stranger and defend the poor. We see others with fearful, possessive eyes. We give up when our compassion is stretched thin by the grief of this world. The wonder we have seen with you is quickly set aside by the burdens of our daily activities. We confess that we have downplayed

imagination and given up its possibilities for furthering your work in new areas. Hear us, gracious God, and forgive us.

Many: God, merciful and loving, long-suffering and abundant in goodness and truth, keeping mercy for millions, forgiving insensitivity, transgressions, and sins;

One: God, who will by no means forgive the unrepentant, listen to our pleas.

Many: For we do not ask for your help because of our goodness, but only because of your great compassion. Hear us, gracious God.

One: Create in us clean hearts, O God, and renew a right spirit within us. Restore the joy of your salvation to us, and uphold us with your living Spirit.

Many: Have mercy upon us, according to your loving kindness, according to the multitude of your tender mercies. Blot out our transgressions, through Jesus Christ, our Savior. Christ, have mercy on us.

One: God says, "I will be merciful to your self-centeredness, and your sins I will not remember. Go and live only for me."

Conversion of Saint Paul

January 25

This is a celebration of Paul's change from being a persecutor of Christianity to becoming one of its leading advocates. His dramatic account of being blinded on the road to Damascus is recorded in Acts 9.

Prayer for the Conversion of Saint Paul

Patient God, when we became Christians, we certainly weren't saints, and yet you call us to become such. As we celebrate Saint Paul's conversion and his movement from judgment to love, let us remember when we first realized we really did believe in you. Help us continue to convert our lives, to draw ever nearer, and to learn more about what it takes to become one of your saints. Amen.

Black History Month

February

Black History Month is a time of paying special tribute to the African American heritage and culture in the United States. The celebration began in 1926 as Negro History Week and is a time of remembering the past, acknowledging the present, and preparing for the future.

On the Sundays of the month, churches can focus on the black church— its West African roots, its development alongside the white church structure, and its impact on black history. Black music can be celebrated, with special attention paid to the variety of music in the black church: spirituals, gospel, and metered hymns. Music and other art forms can be looked at as expressions of worship, art, and protest. Your church may choose to sponsor a black poetry reading or to display tapestries and paintings by black artists on the walls of the sanctuary. Other themes can involve the black family and the development of community resources.

Include preachers and interfaith choirs in your worship service, and invite guests to lead special forums on various topics and community needs. Sponsor a film festival featuring videos on the civil rights movement and other historical themes, or the films of black directors such as Robert Townsend and Spike Lee. Invite black community leaders to talk about their work. Put inserts into your Sunday program that tell about historic events and the lives of black leaders like Carter Godwin Woodson, Mary McLeod Bethune, W. E. B. DuBois, Shirley Chisholm, George Washington Carver, and June Jordan. Meet as a congregation to discuss your church's effectiveness in welcoming, affirming, and involving people of all races.

Because people of African descent have been in the United States for over 350 years, congregations should not attempt to cover all aspects of black history within the month. Rather, some observances should occur throughout the year. The black national anthem, "Lift Every Voice and Sing," by James Weldon and John Rosamond Johnson, is an important part of each year's celebration.

Presentation of Jesus in the Temple (Candlemas)

February 2

According to Luke 2:22, Jesus was presented in the temple forty days after his birth. This festival is also called Candlemas and the purification of Mary. On this date, some churches recall Simeon's words about the Messiah being a light to the Gentiles by blessing their candles during a special candlelight service. This observance celebrates the shift from the old dispensation, represented by Anna and Simeon, to the new dispensation, represented by Jesus.

Litany: In Jesus' Face We See

Luke 2:22–40

One: We have seen the Christ child, and he is beautiful! He is our Savior, Messiah, Redeemer, Guide, Comforter, Challenger, and Teacher. He is our deliverance! But of what? Why are we so happy that Jesus is here?

Many: We want peace and justice for all. We want reconciliation among people. We want forgiveness, guidance, and inspiration. And we want people of all races and nations to see what we see in this child.

One: And what do we see?

Many: We see a need for Jesus to continue the works of creation in the midst of destruction.

We see a need for reconciliation and education in our families and schools, that we may be better parents and children, better teachers and students; that we may bring in peace and justice with our lives.

We see a need for peace among the nations of the world and peace on the streets of our communities.

We see a need for a balanced economy so that there are decent jobs for all people and every person can afford decent shelter, clothing, and food.

We see a need to be as open to people's needs as Jesus is to ours. We want to be able to see Jesus in faces that appear even in unexpected places.

One: In Jesus Simeon saw the hope of the ages. He had steadfastly believed that something would happen before he died, that the Promised One would come, and that the lives of many would be changed for the good.

Many: Anna had maintained a vigil in the Temple for years, believing that someone special would come and that all who looked for their own redemption, as well as that of religion and society, would indeed find it. When she saw Jesus' face, she knew her dreams had been fulfilled.

Prayer for Candlemas

God who does not forget, may we wait patiently for you to come into our lives, especially when our lives aren't going so well. Help us not give up our hope that you will come, even as we grow old. And when you do come, let us see the smiling eyes of your glory in the world, that we may heal some of the brokenness in the world, that our lives may be fulfilled, and that we may die happy. Amen.

Transfiguration

Sunday before Ash Wednesday
The date for this feast on the Episcopal and Catholic calendars is August 6. While the Roman Catholic calendar observes this feast on August 6 alone, the Episcopal calendar observes the feast on both days.

This festival commemorates the time when Jesus took Peter, James, and John to a mountaintop to pray. As the three watched, Jesus' face became radiant with a supernatural light, and Moses and Elijah seemed to be talking with him. Moses stands for the Jewish law, given to him in the form of the Ten Commandments on Mount Sinai; the prophet Elijah, who was expected to reappear just before the Messiah, is a messianic symbol. Jesus then becomes part of the Jewish tradition and completes it.

A Service for the Transfiguration of Jesus

Matthew 17:1–21

CALL TO WORSHIP
Come, all who would see the light and be consumed by it! The God of brilliance waits!

RESPONSIVE READING

One: Today we remember the transfiguration of Jesus on the mountaintop.

Many: What does "transfigure" mean?

One: The light of Jesus' transfiguration, when he stood illuminated with Moses and Elijah and when Peter wanted to build shelters, reveals to us that our buildings, our "holy activities and structures," cannot replace faith or even convince us that we have faith.

Many: We don't understand. You don't want us to build?

One: We are not here to build monuments that are glorious. We are here to transform the world and make its people glorious.

Many: That doesn't sound easy!

One: Listen with me awhile, that we may hear.

PRAYER OF CONFESSION

Dear Friend, we keep looking to you for signs, but when they appear we see but do not understand. We catch a glimpse of your light but then turn away because it is too bright, and we see only a part of your reality. So we build things and stay busy, all the while trying to approximate your glory. If only we would dare to stare into your light, to take the risk of being overcome and transformed, then we could become transparent with your love.

Your light is here. May we look without reserve, believe without needing to understand, and follow without wondering where we are headed. May we believe that you are the One. May we leave the comfort of our shadows behind and walk boldly into the light of faith. Amen.

A reading from Matthew 17:1–21 follows.

PRAYER

God of light, Hope of shadows, let justice shine like a beacon of unfailing light. May the shadows behind our hopes and the fears beneath our dreams give way to life. May your radiance penetrate our hearts so completely, and your fire burn within us so deeply, that we become purified and simplified in our lives. When the shadows come, when the center no longer holds, when all that has been is swept away, may we look for your light. May your image always glow within our eyes, so that even in the gloomiest time, our faces will glow with your light. May this be so.

GOD OF THE NIGHT

I hurry through the burning brightness of each day,
that I might reach the solace of the night.
In the settling of the evening hours,
as shadows deepen into purity,
I calm and find my God.

As the colors of the day come together into blackness,
I begin to feel God's rhythm
and hear the timbre
of God's eternal and compassionate voice.

In the darkness, with the light of day gone,
God's presence comes,
the voices of the world's people are heard
and felt.

In blackness my God lives.

5

~~~

Lent and Easter

Unlike the Christmas season with all its parties, running around, buying presents, baking cookies, and decorating, the season of Lent is a slower time, a time of reflection, self-examination, and commitment. The traditional forty days of Lent offer people a chance to focus on how to live a more Christian life.

Lent (meaning "spring") begins on Ash Wednesday, the Wednesday before the sixth Sunday before Easter. Lent is referred to for the first time by the Council of Nicaea in 325 C.E. as an extended fast before the Passover and as a period of preparation for baptism. The lenten disciplines developed out of this and traditionally include fasting, prayer, the study of scripture, and the giving of alms. Lent is a somber time. In the music of the church, hymns of celebration are set aside until Easter morning.

The actual length of Lent varies considerably depending upon how the forty-day period is calculated. Some traditions do not count Sundays, some do not count Saturdays or Sundays. Some do not include the days of Holy Week while others just include Good Friday and Holy Saturday. Overall, Lent lasts from six to eight weeks.

In the Western Christian tradition, the forty days of Lent begin with Ash Wednesday, exclude Sundays because of their importance in their own right, and include Holy Week. In the Eastern Orthodox tradition, Lent begins on the Monday before Ash Wednesday and continues until the Friday before Palm Sunday, thus excluding Holy Week but including Sundays. For a while in history, a three-week period of preparation preceded Lent. The three pre-lenten Sundays were known as Septuagesima, Sexagesima, and Quinquagesima. The days from Quinquagesima to Ash

Wednesday became the final days of celebration before the fasting of Lent began. Remnants of this tradition can be seen in the Mardi Gras celebrations in New Orleans. Shrove (meaning "Penance") Tuesday, or Fat Tuesday, originated out of this period of festivity, as did the German *fastnacht,* now symbolized by the doughnut.

As the baptismal focus of Lent lessened with the decline of adult baptisms, the penitential character of the season developed. The marking of ashes on Ash Wednesday is one expression of this. Lent's liturgical colors are purple for royalty and violet for penitence. In general there is a muting of colors in Lent to go with the muting of joyous music, until all explodes with the celebration on Easter morning.

In the early church, the Christian Passover celebrated on one day all the events of Jesus' last days. As persecutions lessened and people were free to travel to the Holy Land, this one day of remembrance lengthened into a week of events, as pilgrims retraced Jesus' steps during his last week. The liturgical colors for Holy Week are deep red to symbolize the blood of Jesus, and black for Jesus' death.

Daily devotions are an important part of observing Lent, and the church's worship committee can create meditational materials and instructions to help people find a quiet place to think and reflect.

The Sundays of Lent

Lenten Liturgics

CONFESSION

Joel 2:1–2,12–17

One: Blow the trumpet in Zion! Sanctify a fast! Call a solemn assembly! Gather the people! This is a day of confession, a time to return to God and speak from the depths of our hearts!

Many: We return to God confessing all those matters we have done that we should not have done, and those matters we have left undone which we should have done. We confess that we have doubted our own abilities, not listened to the needs of others, and have preferred to be right rather than to be reconciled.

One: We gather to seek God's understanding and forgiveness.

Many: We confess that too often we live each day off balance, reacting from unsteady nerves rather than from our center. We affirm that God is gracious and merciful, eager to walk with us and listen to the words we speak and the words we leave unspoken. We know that if we confess honestly and are repentant, God will welcome us to the table of fellowship.

CONFRONTATION

Luke 4:1–13

One: In the beginning, God confronted the heavens and the earth.

Many: God saw all that had been confronted, and behold, it was very good.

One: "Confrontation" is another word for creation. When faced with any situation, we can create something positive, or we can run away and let the conflict fester. A confrontation is a period of tension, when a relationship either moves forward and is reborn with more depth and richness or moves backward and begins to die.

Many: We come together each week as a community of believers, not just to hear about God, but also to hear from one another, to grow in fellowship.

One: By confronting what we do not understand, we affirm our commitments. By confronting, we develop community. By confronting, we say that we care about one another.

Many: Let us confront the mysteries within ourselves with honesty, that we may discern who we are, even where uneasy shadows linger. Let us confront one another with openness, that we may share what God has revealed to us. And let us confront God with searching hearts, that we may fully understand what God's love requires us to do.

PRAYER

Zealous Jesus, who took joy in telling everyone about God's wonderful love, we too often take pleasure in being angry and jealous and depressed, because these strong emotions make us feel alive and in control. But we aren't in control much of the time, and these emotions are destructive energies that only pull us down into a whirlpool of pity.

Connect us with the emotions that Jesus felt, ones that create and renew, ones that heal and reconcile—love, joy, gratitude, and hope. Move us beyond our desires to get even. Fire us up so that we will use our energies to be zealous like you. Amen.

Dreams
Genesis 15:1–12, 17–18

One: The old shall see visions! The young shall dream dreams!

Many: And all God's people shall see the glory of God together!

One: This is how God's dreams begin. Those who hold fast to faith, even in troubled times, have visions and catch a glimpse of God's coming world. They see unexpected possibilities that transfigure today's plans.

Many: We know that we don't respond well to the unexpected or to surprises. We like to be safe and warm in our old habits, comfortable in our traditional ways of doing things. But God is always doing something new. We know that God's dreams will lead us into our deserts, where there will be pain and sorrow and discomfort. We know that the desert will transform us. And when it is time, as it was with the people of Israel, God's dreams will eventually lead us into the promised land.

One: Martin said, "Even though we face the difficulties of today and tomorrow, I still have a dream. We've got some difficult days ahead. But I've been to the mountaintop, and I've seen the promised land. Mine eyes have seen the glory of the coming of the Lord."

Many: Spirit of surprises, open up our faith to the unexpected movement of your Spirit in our lives, fill our heads with dreams of what might be, enter our idle thoughts with visions that excite us right down to our toes. O Spirit of newness, nudge us forward into action, into the fire of love, that we might burn with the yearning of all creation for completion. In your name we pray. Amen.

Wilderness
Exodus 3:1–15

One: God says, "Come, follow me. Follow me into the desert, where I will transform you. Follow me into the wilderness, and I will give you rest."

Many: We will follow God, full of faith and conviction. Wherever God leads, we will be there. Wherever God takes us, we will not be afraid.

One: God will take us into the barren desert to confront who we are, to uncover our weaknesses, to discover our abilities, to recover our dreams for ministry.

Many: May our journey through the desert and into the heart of God unite us with Jesus' own sufferings—his poverty, oppression, abandonment, and injustice. From the depths of Jesus' wounds, may we minister with the breadth of Jesus' compassion.

One: We know that our faith will falter now and then. There will be times when we are sure we are all alone. There will be times when we are sure there is no way out. There will be times when we are sure we are going to die. Yet we must not be afraid. We must not give up hope in the face of our troubles.

Many: Nurturing God, whenever days seem too hard for us to bear, calm our anxieties with your touch. Reassure us with the comfort of your presence. Instill in us the courage to stay with you when all we want to do is go home. Fill us up with faith! Do not let us take the easy way out! Amen.

Illusions
2 Corinthians 5:16–21

One: If we are good enough Christians, God will make us rich!

Many: We wish!

One: If we just pray enough, we will never get sick and we will never, ever die!

Many: Really?

One: And people who cheat, lie, and commit horrible acts will all be swiftly and justly punished!

Many: In our lifetimes?

One: Wake up, people! The ways of God are not the ways of this world. God does not measure success in terms of money, possessions, health, or prestige. These worldly successes are illusions, confusions of God's plans. In God's eyes, none of us is better or worse than anyone else.

Many: Then how do we keep score?

One: We are like fig trees planted in God's garden. If we produce figs, then we are successful to God. If we do not, then God will pull us up and toss us on the mulch pile.

Many: What are these figs we are to produce?

One: Wait, and you will hear.

Prayer of Focus

Dear God, help us not be concerned over how well other people seem to be doing. Let us only be concerned about our relationship with you, that we may be productive in ways that matter to you. If we have open hearts, discerning spirits, and lives that are full of compassion, then we will be successful in your eyes. O God, may this be so. Amen.

Priorities
Philippians 3:8–14

One: In the hurry of your lives, you have taken valuable time today to come here and be together. Why?

Many: We want to acknowledge that God is our first priority and affirm that everything we do is based on this commitment.

One: Then let us slow our pace and enter our worship with this singleness of mind.

Many: Amen.

Prayer Litany for Lent

One: O Lamb of God, who takes away the sins of the world,

Many: Give us your peace.
        Pause.

One: Dear God, Creator of the world, you revealed your great love for us by sending your Child into the world to be the sacrifice that cancels our sins and allows us to be one with you. With joy, we give you thanks for rescuing us from the power of the shadows, encouraging us to be part of your people of light, and bringing us safely into the family of Jesus.

Many: Through Jesus we are set free, through the forgiveness of our sins.
        Pause.

One: Dear God, Redeemer of the world, you had the nature of God and became human. You walked the path of obedience all the way to your death on the cross.

Many: Compel us by your love to live from now on, not for ourselves, but for you.
        Pause.

One: We give you thanks that you became one of us in every way. You were despised and rejected. You suffered and endured pain. Because of our sins, you were tortured, beaten, and killed.

Many: We are healed because of your wounds, made whole because you received our punishment.
Pause.

One: Dear God, Sustainer of the world, you who are united with the Mother/Father and the Christ, we give you thanks that you descended upon Jesus and empowered him to bring the good news to the poor, to heal the brokenhearted, to set free the oppressed, to announce release to the captives and recovery of sight to the blind, and to declare that the time had finally come when God would save the people.

Many: Pour this love of God into our hearts, that we may minister as Jesus did.
Pause.

One: From the sin of unbelief, from all misuse of our lives, from all self-righteousness, from every neglect of our duty, from all ingratitude and selfishness, from apathy, from indifference toward your meritorious life and death,

Many: Deliver us, gracious God.
Pause.

One: Because you became human, because you endured hardships without resentment, because you remained faithful to your mission on earth even when you could have chosen to go elsewhere, we are able to live again.

Many: Receive us, dear God.
Pause.

One: Because you rose from the dead, because you came back and spoke words of comfort and direction to your disciples, because you sent the Spirit to be with us always, we are able to go to others with your power to comfort and heal.

Many: Empower us, dear God, to be your disciples.
Pause.

One: That we may bear this love to others,

Many: That we may witness to our crucified and risen Jesus,

All: We confess our faith in your boundless love, O God.

A Kiowa Prayer of Our Savior

Inspired by a Kiowa translation

> God, you who are the Creator of all the world,
> who lives above us beyond the clouds and sky,
> who lives around us in the mountains and woods,
> who lives beneath us in the earth and water,
> we honor your name.
>
> May what you want to be done here among us
> be carried on the winds to all the tribes,
> to all the creatures of the earth,
> who live in the four directions.
>
> Give us a successful hunt, that we may not starve,
> that we will have warm clothing for our backs
> and strong shelter for our families.
>
> Forgive us when we forget your way,
> when we neglect to honor you with our dance,
> or treat each part of your creation with respect,
> or listen to the visions your Spirit sends,
> as we forgive those who break our traditions.
>
> Keep us from stealing the souls of others.
> Take trouble far away from our hearts.
> Set us free from the evil one.
> All belongs to you—the horse and the buffalo,
> the rains and the prairie grass,
> the eagle and the deer.
> All praise and wonder we offer to you,
> from the dawning of the sun until forever.

Ash Wednesday

Lent formally begins on Ash Wednesday, when Christians confess their sins, accept forgiveness, and receive a mark of ashes on their foreheads as a sign of their repentance. This is the fortieth day before Easter. The ashes are prepared by burning palms from the preceding year's Palm Sunday. The marking is done as a symbol of the penitential character of the lenten season and serves as a reminder of one's mortality and an exhortation to be faithful to the gospel. The idea for the service comes from Old Testament times, when mourners and penitents clothed themselves in sackcloth and sprinkled their heads and faces with dust or ashes as a sign that they were sorry for something they either had done or had failed to do.

Ash Wednesday Penance Service

CALL TO WORSHIP
Isaiah 51

> Listen. Listen to me.
> Listen and you shall live!
> Pay attention, and come to me.
> Come and you shall live.

Meditative music is played, such as "Come to the Water" by John Foley, St. Louis Jesuits.

FIRST READING
Joel 2:1–2, 12–17a
One: Return to God and repent.
             All pray quietly.

SECOND READING
Psalm 51:1–12
One: Have mercy on me, O God, a sinner.
A period of quiet prayer is followed by meditative music, such as "What You Hear in the Dark," by Dan Schutte, St. Louis Jesuits.

UNISON PRAYER
Merciful God, we come to you today realizing that we are not who you want us to be. Help us let go of our past, that we may turn toward you and live again the life of faith. Help us call out our fear and hatred, our anger and self-pity. Lift the burden these negative emotions place on our shoulders. Help us set aside our guilt and enter a season of healing. As we pray and fast today, help us become simple people, that we may see you plainly. As we wear the mark of ashes, rekindle the sign of hope within our eyes. Let us draw near to you now. Amen.

COLLECTION OF SINS
Take a piece of paper from the offering plate. Write on it what you would like God's forgiveness for today. No one will read what you write. When everyone is finished, the papers will be collected. A period of quiet meditation follows.

THIRD READING
2 Corinthians 5:20b–6:2
One: Be reconciled to God, you who have confessed your sins.

PRAYER OF THE CONGREGATION
Anyone who wants to may offer a one-sentence prayer. After each sentence, the congregation responds, "God, hear our prayer."

THE BURNING OF SINS, THE BLESSING AND DISTRIBUTION OF ASHES
The collected papers are burned, and the congregation comes up the center aisle to the front. As the mark of ashes is made on each person's forehead, he or she is asked, "Will you turn away from sin and respond to the gospel?" Each penitent responds with an affirmation and returns to his or her seat.

Meditative music is played, such as "Hosea," by Weston Priory.

EXCHANGE OF PEACE

Quietly offer these words to the people around you: "May God be with you." Respond: "And also with you."

DISMISSAL PRAYER

We have come before God and confessed our sorrow and despair. We have allowed the mark of ashes to be placed on our foreheads so that the world will know that we are in mourning for our lives. We have relinquished the ownership of our failings and let God take the burden of them away. And we have resolved to live life free of our past, following only the dreams that God sends us.

Go now into the world with the assurance of hope in your hearts. Go now and live for God's sake. Go now and live free. Amen.

As the prayer concludes and the service ends, congregants may stay in the sanctuary as long as they like—to pray, think, or just sit. When they leave, they should do so quietly.

Palm/Passion Sunday

Matthew 21:1–17; Mark 11:1–19; Luke 19:29–46; John 12:12–50
The events of Jesus' last week are described in detail by the gospel writers. Members of the congregation can come together each evening during the week to read the scriptures for the day, to pray, and to discuss what has been read. They may meet at the church or in people's homes.

Holy Week begins with Palm, or Passion, Sunday. "Palm" refers to the joyous waving of palm branches during Jesus' entry into Jerusalem on this day, and "passion" because the gospel story for the day tells about Jesus' passions during his last week of human life: the agony in Gethsemane, the betrayal and arrest, the hearings and trials, the scourging and mocking, the carrying of the cross to Calvary, and the crucifixion and death. Some churches focus on Jesus' entry into Jerusalem on Palm Sunday, and read the rest of the story during corresponding days of Holy Week. Many churches process into the sanctuary on Palm Sunday waving palms.

Suffering

Isaiah 52:7–10

One: How beautiful upon the mountains are the feet of the messenger who brings good news, who announces peace, who proclaims salvation, who says to Zion, "Your God reigns!"

Many: Listen! Our sentinels shout from the city walls! Together they sing for joy! For in plain sight they see God returning to Zion!

One: But the messenger who comes is not the one expected. There are no trumpets of grandeur. Jesus isn't riding in on a big white horse; he's riding in on a small donkey. He isn't marching up to sit on his royal throne; he's walking forward to hang on a wooden cross. He comes as one who will end up suffering for us and who will heal us with his wounded hands.

Many: And we will be called to follow in his footsteps, to remain faithful in the midst of suffering. In this way we will discover the joys and strengths of Christ within us. In this way we will find our own words and actions to bear witness to the good news of Christ.

One: There is no rationalizing today's suffering. There is no forgetting the sorrow that has been ours in the past. There is no avoiding the persecutions that will come, if we are true to the gospel. Suffering is a part of life, and by embracing the suffering that is ours, by bringing meaning to today's events, we join the mighty cloud of witnesses who have gone on before us!

Many: Break forth into singing, you ruins of Jerusalem! God is coming to comfort and redeem! We will stand and sing of our faith! And all the earth shall see the salvation of our God! Amen!

Monday of Holy Week

Matthew 21:18–23:39; Mark 11:20–13:37; Luke 19:47–21:36

Prayer for Monday of Holy Week

On the day after the glorious Palm Sunday parade, the debate begins. The religious authorities ask Jesus pointed questions in order to judge the "correctness" of his theology. Jesus responds by telling them stories that sidestep the legalities but speak of a deeper wisdom. Then he asks the crowd why they haven't listened to the prophets and why the prophets seem to die in their city so often.

We have our standards, God, and woe to anyone who crosses the line of what we think is acceptable. Like the religious authorities, we will persecute those who work outside the boundaries. And like the people of Jerusalem, we will stone those who upset the usual order of our day. We don't want to be like this, so judgmental all the time. When we come across those we don't understand, we want to be able to listen with open minds and hear with open hearts. Help us, O God, to always be willing to learn more about your world. Amen.

Tuesday of Holy Week

Matthew 24:1–26:5; Mark 14:1–11; Luke 21:36–22:6

Prayer for Tuesday of Holy Week

The next day the disciples ask their question, mostly about what will happen next. Even though Jesus tells them, their understanding is limited by unrealistic expectations. So he tells them stories, which only seem to confuse them more. Meanwhile, the religious leaders, having realized the meaning of Jesus' words to them, create a plan to undermine his movement.

God, we have built temples around what is familiar in our lives and walls around the temples. We have set expectations for how life will run its course. And we have built up hopes and dreams to get us through the rough times, even if they aren't always constructive. It is so hard, God, to let go of these supports and turn everything over to you. We don't like to live day to day, simply doing what we can for the people we meet. We like to have grand goals to work toward, with detailed plans of what we'll do every day and massive amounts of resources to throw into our projects. It is hard to live each day with only the goal of helping the people we meet and using only the resources we carry in our coat pockets. Help us to listen carefully to you so that we will hear the right words to speak to the person waiting in front of us. Amen.

Wednesday of Holy Week

Matthew 26:6–16
Wednesday is the only day in Jesus' last week on earth when the Gospel writers are vague about his activities. Since some of the readings for Holy Week are long and some duplicate others, you may choose to spread out the readings from the early part of the week so that there is something to read on Wednesday. Or read the Matthew passage noted above and have a service of quiet meditation on the woman's insight about Jesus.

SEVEN ELEMENTS MEDITATION

Wednesday of Holy Week seems to have been a quiet day for Jesus, perhaps one of retreat and preparation for the string of events that were to begin on Thursday. The gospel writers are all silent except Matthew, and the events he describes in 26:6–16 may actually have happened on Tuesday. This passage touches on a number of themes. Jesus enters the house of an unclean person, a leper. A woman "wastes" expensive perfume on him. The disciples get angry. Jesus says that the poor are always with us but that he will not be. He speaks of preparing for burial, and that the good news is to be proclaimed. Judas, for his reasons, seeks to force Jesus' hand by betraying him. All of these themes are worthy of meditation. This service can either be a personal meditation or one done in groups.

There are a few objects to collect before the service begins: a candle, two large bowls, warm water, a ceramic cup, salt, a package of yeast, a saucer, a prism, a piece of bread, a bell, and woven fabric. Place the two large bowls in front of you—one empty and the other filled with water.

Just before sunset, sit down in your meditation place. Watch the light shift and the sky darken as the sun goes down. Then light a candle and begin the meditations. You may want to burn incense, reminiscent of the more liturgical Christian churches, or sage, used by American Indians for purification. After each meditation, listen to the changing sounds as you slowly pour a cup of water from one bowl into the other. Keep a notebook nearby to write down your thoughts.

MEDITATIONS

It is necessary to stay here, unseeing, feeling nothing, being obedient to faith, until the time when the sweetness of God's presence comes. Do not seek to fill this void, because only God can fill it. It is necessary to leave all thoughts behind because God is beyond thought; to leave all feelings behind, even though feelings come closer to God because they come from our hearts. What we are instructed to do is to stay here and wait.

When was the last time you shared your struggles of faith with a Christian neighbor over the back fence? Or shared the good news with a stranger when the opportunity presented itself? What did you say? Was there anything you wished you had said?

Salt

Pour salt into the palm of your hand. Look at its crystals closely. Smell it. Taste it.

We are to be as salt to the world, but if we have lost our saltiness, then what are we good for, except to be thrown out? If we call ourselves Christians but no one else knows this, then God's love ends with us. Salt, like bread, is essential to life. Beyond this, salt and other spices make food worth eating. Variety and pleasure are a part of living. We are to be like salsa in the world, livening things up, providing zing! We are to inspire people to sit up and take notice. Life without salsa is bland and tasteless. Life without spice can lead to despair.

How are you like salt/salsa in the world?

Leaven

Pour one-fourth cup warm water into the saucer and sprinkle the yeast over it. Watch it and smell it.

We are to be as leaven in the dough, stirring things up, getting things going. We are to move into the unmoving, despairing masses and help things develop, that we all may rise and become everything that lies in wait, in promise, within us. We are to join the rhythm, the pulsing of God's love throughout the world, moving with our bodies, our emotions, and our minds, celebrating the physicality of life and the sheer joy of being alive. Yet, like salt, what good is yeast if it has been activated but not used?

What do you make happen that wouldn't happen if you weren't around?

Light

Hold a prism up to the candlelight. Watch the colors come out. Some have compared light to God's love, the prism to Jesus, and the rainbow colors to the diversity of people's love in the world.

We are to be light for the world, a beacon on the hill for those seeking help, like the neon cross on the homeless shelter which shines for those whose eyes and minds are dimmed by addiction and despair. We are to be colors in the world, the red-green-black, the rainbow colors, which, like spices, transform what is bland into something exciting. We are the banners of God flying in the winds of everyday challenges, the prayer wheels that spin around in the breeze announcing God's endless hope and loving. We are the smiles of God beaming toward others. We are those who walk with a bounce in our step that says "Life is good!" We are those who walk our talk.

What inspires you like seeing a beacon in the night? How are you struggling to live out your faith more fully?

Earth/Pottery

Take the ceramic cup. Turn it around in your hands. Feel its rough surfaces, its jagged edges, and the unevenness of its glaze.

God is like a potter who is constantly molding and shaping us. We are not yet complete or finished. The process continues. Our lives are being shaped by God's hands. Sometimes God lets go of our clay to see if we are ready, to see whether we will keep the shape God wants for us or whether we will begin to fly off the potter's wheel like Judas. When we finally hold the shape God intends for us, we're put into the kiln of trials and baked into something solid and useful. Yet we are delicate earthen vessels entrusted with a priceless treasure.

How is God shaping you?

Bread

Pick up the bread. Smell it. Break off a piece, put it in your mouth and taste its goodness. Think of the fields where the grain was grown.

We are bread for the world, the staff of life providing needed nutrients. Like Jesus, we are called to be as bread broken for others, consumed in the giving of ourselves to the needs of others. The smell of bread baking reminds us of the joy of sharing together in community, of praying together, of going to the work that is our ministry. The bread broken in communion makes all things possible.

How are you being broken like bread in order to share the good news?

If you would like to, now make a loaf of bread with the yeast you have prepared. Think about how our community is like bread. The bread can be used for Maundy Thursday communion or given to the hungry in the community.

Refined Metal

Pick up a bell. Slide your hands over its surface. Rap it with your knuckle and listen to its sound.

We are like ore that God has gathered from the earth and refined in the fire. Slowly our selfishness and impurities burn off until only the purity of our metal, the purity of God's spirit, remains in us, and we are left so in touch with God's spirit that we can intuit what God would have us do. We ring with God's sound. We respond instinctively with the right words to comfort the grieving and with the right actions to help those in need.

Write down an instance when you responded instinctively to someone's need and felt God's love move through you.

Plants/Thread
Take a piece of woven cloth. With your hands, pull it in opposite directions and feel the combined strength of its threads. With your fingers, explore its edges and holes. Place it on your lap and feel its warmth.

We are as threads woven together by God, who takes our scattered, frayed pieces and makes of them a blanket that covers the world with a warming love. During the night, we hear the Weaver gathering the remnant people of faith from around the world. During the day, we hear the sound of the loom's shuttle going back and forth and the bar bringing us tightly together.

What are the strengths of our community? Where are our holes? What liberation do you seek? What is your prayer for this Easter?

Maundy Thursday

Matthew 26:17–75; Mark 14:12–72; Luke 22:7–65; John 13:1–18:27
Maundy Thursday is a commemoration of the Last Supper and a reconciliation of today's Christians. It was on Thursday night that Jesus gathered with the disciples in the upper room to share the *Seder* meal and celebrate the Jewish Passover. After the meal, Jesus gathered a towel about him and washed the disciples' feet. "Maundy" is from the Latin *mandatum,* which means a new commandment. It refers to Jesus' demonstration to the disciples that their ministries would involve becoming servants. Often all decorations are removed after this liturgy in preparation for the events of Good Friday.

Jesus performs two services on Maundy Thursday, and they are connected. We tend to remember the first (Holy Communion) and think of the second (foot washing) as a cute story.

Christian denominations have gone into war over the correct interpretation and observance of Holy Communion. Some celebrate it monthly, some in every service. Some use wine; others use juice. Some view the elements as the very body of Christ, others as parts of a memorial.

With the second service, foot washing, Jesus shows clearly that this is how we are to live—by serving others. Yet rarely are foot washing services celebrated.

Communion Service: A Reflection on This Communion

(The bread meditation and music are by Kay Ward; wine meditation is by Mark Liebenow.)

A guitar is strummed/picked throughout.

Reader 1: God, in a world of processed everything, we long to look beyond this package of flour to fields of golden wheat—to that basic seed which enables the miracle of life.

Reader 2: "Very truly I tell you, unless a grain of wheat falls into the earth and dies, it remains just a single grain; but if it dies, it bears much fruit. Those who love their life lose it, and those who hate their life in this world will keep it for eternal life" (John 12:24–25).

```
        C    E    G    F    F E D    D    D E D C
```
Sung: Bread made from wheat full of life, God, we thank you.
```
        C         F         G7              C
```

Reader 1: To the flour we add water and are reminded of our need for it and for that living water which can quench our spiritual thirst.

Reader 2: John 4:13-14: Jesus said to her, "Everyone who drinks of this water will be thirsty again, but those who drink of the water that I will give them will never be thirsty. The water that I will give will become in them a spring of water gushing up to eternal life."

Sung: Bread made with water full of life, God, we thank you.

Reader 1: We add the needed salt, for without it, bread remains unsatisfying, tasteless—like a life without shouting the good news.

Reader 2: "You are the salt of the earth; but if salt has lost its taste, how can its saltiness be restored? It is no longer good for anything, but is thrown out and trampled under foot" (Matt. 5:13).

Sung: Bread made with salt full of life, God, we thank you.

Reader 1: God, these three things would lie dormant and never fulfill their potential of becoming bread, we know, without ferment. This is like our lives; for as we become the leaven of our community, we enable it to grow.

Reader 2:   "The realm of heaven is like yeast that a woman took and mixed in with half three measures of flour until all of it was leavened" (Matt. 13:33).

Sung: Bread made with yeast full of life, God, we thank you.

Reader 1:   Carefully combined, these four ingredients become bread. At first the dough is a cumbersome lump, but as we knead and pull, it magically yields itself into one unit—into that thing of extra-ordinariness—bread!

Reader 2:   Jesus said to them, "I am the bread of life. Whoever comes to me will never be hungry, and whoever believes in me will never be thirsty" (John 6:35).

Sung: Bread made from these become one, God, we thank you.
Share the bread with those gathered.

Reader 1:   God, we long to look beyond this wine to the sun-swept hills of purple grapes, to the presses that squeeze out the juice. You are like that, God, and we are your grapes.

Reader 2:   "I am the true vine, and the One who sent me is the vine grower. God removes every branch in me that bears no fruit. Every branch that bears fruit God prunes to make it bear more fruit" (John 15:1–2).

Sung: Wine made from grapes full of life, God, we thank you.

Reader 1:   To the juice we add water. We are reminded that water is the blood of all life and that we need the living water to quench our spiritual thirst.

Reader 2:   And Jesus said, "Whoever gives even a cup of cold water to one of these little ones in the name of a disciple—truly I tell you, none of these will lose their reward" (Matt. 10:42).

Sung: Wine made with water full of life, God, we thank you.

Reader 1:   To this liquid, we add a little sweetness and a little yeast. Without these two things, the wine is bitter and pale. It cannot be used.

Reader 2:   "You were running well; who prevented you from obeying the truth? Such persuasion does not come from the one who calls you. A little yeast leavens the whole batch" (Gal. 5:7–9).

Sung: Wine made with yeast full of life, God, we thank you.

Reader 1: God, just like our lives, without fermentation these things would lie dormant and never become what they are supposed to be. As the juice turns into the more precious wine, so do we turn from sinful people to people united with God.

Reader 2: "Beware, keep alert, for you do not know when the time will come. . . . You do not know when the owner of the house will come" (Mark 13:33, 35).

Sung: Wine made with time full of life, God, we thank you.
Share the wine with those gathered.

Reader 1: This is bread, and this is wine. It is given as a symbol of our oneness, our common experience. In our sharing, may you feel a wholeness in accepting this bread and wine as symbols of the gift God has provided in Jesus the Christ.

	C	E	G	F	A	C	B	B	G	E
Sung:	Life given to you, made with love, made with friends.
	C			F			G7			Am

	A	G	F	E	G	G	FE	D	C
	God, we thank you. God, we accept you now.
	F		C	G7		G		C

Foot Washing

A foot washing service is logistically difficult if people are sitting in unmovable pews. If possible, select a room where the chairs can be arranged either in one large circle or in several smaller circles of eight chairs or so. Communion can be celebrated in the first part of the service. Then, one by one, each person removes the shoes and socks of the person in the next chair, washes his or her feet, and replaces the socks and shoes. Then that person gets up and washes the next person's feet. Prayers and hymns may be offered during the foot washing. Whoever washes the pianist's feet may be in for a challenge, though. An open microphone can be provided, in the Quaker style, for people who are moved by the Spirit to say something about foot washing or the ministry of service.

One: One of the traditions in the Middle East in Jesus' day was for servants to wash the feet of guests when they arrived. Since roads were dusty and people wore sandals, this washing served a practical purpose and made the guests more comfortable. Today our feet don't get as dirty. But after a long day at work, having your feet washed feels wonderful. Listen to the words in John 13:3–20.

The scripture is read and the washing of feet begins.

Jesus' invitation to us is not only to share in the good will of communion but also to do something with the commitment we have just made, which is to live in God's way, to live in service to others. Go and do for others as you have done here.

Good Friday

Matthew 27:1–61; Mark 15:1–47; Luke 22:66–23:56; John 18:28–19:42

By the fourth century, the church was observing Good Friday with a three-hour service of readings and hymns, starting at midday. Various churches in a community often sponsor a joint ecumenical service in which the last seven words or sentences of Jesus from the cross are the focus of short meditations.

Tenebrae is a solemn observance of Holy Communion using candles and scripture. It dramatizes the gathering gloom of Jesus' betrayal and crucifixion. As the accounts are read, the candles are snuffed out one by one until the sanctuary is dark. The worshipers then depart in silence.

Loneliness Litany

Matthew 3:1–3; Psalm 38

Reader 1: John the Baptist appeared as Isaiah predicted, "a voice crying out in the wilderness: 'Prepare the way of the Savior!'"

Reader 2: A voice crying out in the wilderness, proclaiming that Jesus was coming. John's calling is also our longing. A voice crying out from his loneliness on the cross. Jesus' calling is also our calling—a prayer from one who felt alone and uncertain about what was happening.

Reader 1: In the wilderness, we face our doubts in all their terror. If God exists, why do we feel this unquenchable longing? Why do such pain and suffering exist? If there is no God, what are we to do with our longing? How do we make sense of so much horrible senselessness in the world?

Reader 2: The words of the ancient psalmist sound their way down into our untouched hollows: "We are utterly spent and crushed; we groan because of the tumult of our hearts."

Reader 1: We live with one foot in this world and one in God's. We are unwilling to put both feet back into the world and be overrun with gathering despair. Yet we are unable to convince both our feet to move into God's world, because then we would have to live like John.

Reader 2: The words of the ancient psalmist express our despair: "O God, all our longing is known to you; our sighing is not hidden from you!"

Reader 1: In moments of solitude, when our faith seems to echo in empty cathedrals, the words of the psalmist cry out in the night and haunt our dreams: "As for the light of our eyes, it also has gone. O God, do not be far from us!"

Reader 2: In our anguish, we turn to our loneliness. We sense that through this searching, we will find the path that Isaiah predicted, the path that John proclaimed, the path that Martin said would lead us to God. "O God, our salvation!"

Reader 1: Our sadness becomes a prayer and joins the psalmist's calling and the prophet's cries. They despaired yet held on to the hope that beyond all suffering, beyond all loneliness, beyond all terror God would be ever faithful. God hears our cries and will send us comfort.

Reader 2: John prepared the way for Christ. We need to receive that way into our lives and prepare the way for others.

Reader 1: The unquenchable longing we feel is also God's longing for us.

Holy Saturday/Easter Eve

Matthew 26:62–66

The nightlong vigil on Holy Saturday, which features fasting and a review of the whole history of salvation, ends, in some traditions, after midnight; in others, it ends with the rising of the sun. Jesus' resurrection on Easter morning is then joyously celebrated. Some traditions forgo the Saturday vigil and go to bed early, getting up before dawn to process silently to a cemetery, where a service is held and brass instruments sing out the good news.

The vigil is a service of fasting, of words and silence, of candlelight and darkness, of sitting and meditative prayer. The vigil can be of any length. Some services start at sunset and last until just after midnight. Others continue until dawn and break the fast with a simple meal. Allow time between readings for silence, prayer, and hymn singing.

Baptisms historically took place on Holy Saturday as converts were initiated into the Christian mystery. Foot washing was also common as a way of affirming the servant nature of Christian living. The imagery of new light about to enter the world is marked by the lighting of the Christian Passover candle and the blessing of new fire.

Water and Fire Service

A day of fasting is observed in preparation for the service.

GREETING

One: God be with you.

Many: And also with you.

One: Lift up your hearts, minds, and souls to God.

Many: It is good to lift up all that we are to God as an offering.

One: Give thanks to God the Almighty.

Many: It is right to give God our thanks and praise.

SERVICE OF THE WORD

We gather tonight to remember how God has been with us since the beginning, and to prepare for the fulfillment of God's promise in the events of Easter morning.

Each of the following readings is followed by a prayer and a hymn:

1. Genesis 1:1, 26–31 (creation).

2. Genesis 17:1–8 (covenant with Abraham).

3. Genesis 22:1–18 (sacrifice of Isaac).

4. Exodus 14:21–29 (Moses and the Red Sea).

5. Isaiah 55:1–11 (come, all who hunger).

6. Micah 6:8 (what God requires of us).

7. Mark 8:1–10 (miracle of the loaves and fish).

8. Mark 9:1–13 (transfiguration).

9. Romans 6:3–11 (we die and rise with Christ).

10. John 1:1–5 (Jesus as the Word).

SERVICE OF WATER

Pouring and Blessing of the Water
We realize the importance of water in our world. We remember the waters of creation, of birth, and of baptism—dying to what has been and being born into the new.

Renewal of Baptismal Vows

One: Do you affirm your renunciation of evil, of selfishness and greed, and renew your commitment to follow Jesus Christ?

Many: We do.

One: Do you believe in God the Almighty?

Many: We believe in God, the Creator of heaven and earth.

One: Do you believe in Jesus Christ?

Many: We believe in Jesus the Christ, the One sent from God, who was with God in the beginning and who has died that we might be free.

One: Do you believe in the Holy Spirit?

Many: We believe in God the Holy Spirit, who guides us and teaches us how to live.

One:	Will you continue in the apostles' teaching and community, in prayer and fellowship, and in the breaking of bread and sharing of wine?
Many:	We will, with the help of God and one another.
One:	Will you strive for justice and peace among all people, respecting the dignity of every human being and the sacredness of all God's creation?
Many:	We will, with the help of God and one another.

Blessing of the People

May this mark of water on your forehead remind you of your baptism and your commitment to live no longer for yourself, but only for God in all that you think, feel, say, and do.

A hymn is sung, such as "Comin' Home," by Tom Hunter.

SERVICE OF LIGHT

Blessing of New Fire

A large bowl filled with coals or slow-burning wood chips is lighted.

For centuries, God guided the people of Israel, sometimes appearing in a burning bush, sometimes as a pillar of fire. Yet the confusion in people's minds continued. So God sent Jesus to show them how to live a life of faith, a life in constant communion with God. Jesus is our new light, a light about to rise over the world. Amen.

The reading of John 1:6–18 (Jesus as the coming of the light) is followed by the lighting of the Paschal (Christian Passover) candle. Then songs, prayers, and scriptural readings continue until midnight or dawn.

Easter Sunday

Matthew 28:1–20; Mark 16:1–20; Luke 24:1–53; John 20:1–31

Service of Easter Dawn

A reading from Luke 24:1–53 retells the events of the first Easter morning.

One:	Alleluia! Christ is risen.
Many:	Christ is risen indeed! Alleluia!

Easter Dawn

The air is cool and hesitant. Stars twinkle out slowly as the night sky gives way to the gray promise of the rising sun. Feelings of longing, of belief, and of hope fill my body and unite to surge with an unspeakable joy. Expectant grays give way to pinks, oranges, and yellows as the sun slowly rises over the still-shadowy trees. People gather. The sky deepens into blue, and birds rise into the air with slow, sure strokes, soaring toward the unknowable Presence.

> It is a celebration.
> The unsubtle coming of Jesus into my life
> with life,
> and his quiet movement into my past
> to heal the hurts
> and the fears;
> a touch that shapes with gentleness,
> directs with firmness,
> and upholds with love.
> It is the proclamation of love
> spoken with our lives.
> And it is a longing to be touched again,
> more deeply . . .
> Easter!

Psalm 118:14–24 is read.

One: Let everyone rejoice! Sing, choirs of angels!
Many: Jesus has passed from death to life!
One: Jesus the Christ, our light, has risen!
Many: Jesus Christ is risen indeed!

A hymn of celebration is sung, and all enjoy a community meal and the breaking of the fast.

6

≈≈

Eastertide

It was significant to the early Christians that Jesus was crucified at Passover time, when Jews were remembering how God had delivered their ancestors from slavery in Egypt and brought them to the promised land. The Christians realized that they had reached their promised land with Jesus' resurrection. They now could pass over from death into eternal life. The deliverance promised by the Old Testament had now reached its fulfillment in the gospel of the New Testament. Each Sunday became a little Easter—a weekly remembrance of Jesus' resurrection—as well as a weekly reminder that they were to be servants in Christ's name.

The forty days of preparation for Easter is followed by the fifty days of Eastertide rejoicing. These fifty days constitute the oldest season of the church's year and end with the day of Pentecost, when the Holy Spirit came down upon the disciples and followers. For the first three centuries, this season was the only festival observed by all Christians. Christmas was not observed on December 25 until the fourth century.

The date of Pentecost, which occurs within Eastertide, depends upon the date of Easter. Easter falls somewhere between March 23 and April 25, and Pentecost follows fifty days later, between May 11 and June 13. This means that only the days between April 26 and May 10 are part of Eastertide every year. The only special church day is Ascension Sunday, which is the sixth Sunday after Easter and the Sunday before Pentecost.

The ascension of Jesus was originally remembered both on Easter Sunday and on the fiftieth day after Easter. In the fourth century, as the focus on the Holy Spirit led to the development of the theology of the Trinity, the fortieth day after Easter became the day of Jesus' ascension and the sixth Sunday after Easter became Ascension Sunday. The seventh Sunday after Easter remained Pentecost Sunday, and the eighth became Trinity Sunday. These three consecutive Sundays commemorate a major theological development in the Christian church. The colors of Eastertide are white, trimmed with gold.

Central America Sunday

Sunday before March 24

A Service for Central America Sunday

"Some want to keep a gospel so disembodied that it doesn't get involved at all in the world it must save. Christ is now in history. . . . Christ is now bringing about the new heavens and the new earth" (Archbishop Oscar Romero).

CALL TO WORSHIP

One: In truth, I tell you, a grain of wheat remains a solitary grain unless it falls into the earth and dies. But if it dies, it bears a rich harvest. The people who love themselves are lost. Today we remember those who bear the message of Christ in Central America.

Many: They live in torn countries and try to bring hope to the people. They do it not for their own glory, but for God's. They see the need, and their hearts are moved. And although they know that they might be killed, as others have been killed before them, they still serve. They feel they can do no less.

One: Jesus says, "Whoever would serve me, must follow me. Where I am, my servants will be. Whoever serves me will be honored by God. Now my soul is in turmoil, and what am I to say? God, save me from this hour? No. It was for this that I came to this hour."

Many: They work and live with the poor, doing what they can to relieve the misery and terror of daily life. Christ hears the cry of the poor!

One: Blessed be Jesus the Christ! God will lift up every crushed spirit, and in God's loving arms every fear will be calmed!

Many: We know that those who die in Christ's name do not die in vain. They go before us to prepare a place. But they are also with us, helping us to hear the depth of Christ's challenge, daring us to embody God's Word with our lives, showing us how to hope when the world around us becomes a hell.

LITANY OF COMMITMENT

One: How can we offer God thanks for our lives if we do not go to those whose hearts are heavy and whose lives are broken, offering them the faith that we bear in Christ's name? The harvest is plentiful. The laborers are few. Come with me into the fields.

Many: We remember today the witness of Oscar Romero, Archbishop of El Salvador, who said that what was spoken in church must find action in our lives. He continued to preach peace to all sides of the warring factions even after numerous death threats. Then he was gunned down in the midst of celebrating Holy Communion.

One: Our arms will grow weary and our shoes will wear thin, but we will follow our God throughout the world.

Many: We believe in history. The world is not a roll of dice. A new world has begun with Christ! Beyond the difficulties of our existence lives an eternal alleluia! We know that God dries the tears of the oppressed and comforts those in sorrow. Christ, teach us to give voice to this new life in the world.

One: May we, like Oscar Romero, speak out against injustice. May we object with our lives to murder, to torture, and to terror that picks away at the hopes of people. And let us invite others to stand beside us.

All: May Almighty God bless us: God who created us, Jesus who saves us, and the Spirit who sets us free! Amen.

Spring Planting

The Rice Liturgy

> They will not hurt or destroy
> on all my holy mountain;
> for the earth will be full
> of the knowledge of God
> as the waters cover the sea (Isa. 11:9).

Reader 1: In Asia, each village works together for its rice. Much labor is required of the people. But in working so closely together in planning, planting, tending, and harvesting the rice, the people grow close to their neighbors. And because they have to trust one another in order to have food, the people also learn to trust one another with their lives.

Reader 2: As they work with the earth and water and rice, the people become close to nature and to the spirit, the kami, that unites all life. What is not done in common does not last and falls away. If the people do not work together, the work will not get done, for individuals cannot do it on their own. Then, when the first rice is harvested, the entire village celebrates together. After having worked long and hard together, the celebration is a deep and joyous one, full of thanks and cheer and good will.

Reader 1: Spirit from the mountain,
come down to us.
Earth and water,
receive this life.
Rice from our hands,
be rooted and grow.
Mountain *kami* in all.

Reader 3: If we have life, we have life together. If we try to survive apart from one another, we only survive, and our work and our lives come to nothing. We live in a village of faith. If our dreams are to come true, if our lives are to be complete, then we must be part of one another's lives, taking care that only out of our relationship comes our work. We need to profess and live out each day our faith in God, our faith in one another, and our faith in life. We need one another—to plant fields of cooperation, to tend dreams of hope, to celebrate the harvests of justice.

Reader 4: We have never lived in isolation, except in our fears. And we do not worship God by ourselves, but only by holding on to the hands of those around us. If we have faith, we are rooted together. Our individual prayers are but a prelude to communal prayer, and our coming together to plant the fields is but the prelude to the harvest feast. Let us dream and work together. Let us be one with the Spirit, who brings life down from the mountains every spring and returns there every winter to ready new life.

Reader 1: If we have life, we have life together.

Reader 2: If our dreams are to come true, we need one another,

Reader 3: To plant those dreams, to bring deeper visions,

Reader 4: To involve many hands.

Reader 1: We do not live in isolation.

Reader 2: We do not worship by ourselves.

Reader 3: We worship together.

Reader 4: Let us dream and work,

All: As one with this Spirit.

Holy Fools' Day

Sunday before April 1

Fools' Liturgy

(For Christians and other clowns; dedicated to David and Mel Henkelmann.)

CALL TO WORSHIP

Come, you who are tired of holding the world together.
Come, you who are weary of trying to make life make sense.
Come, you who want to dance but can't find the time.

And come, you who are too busy to care for people.
Hey, what are you in this world for?

PRAYER

Funny God, with the sound of your laughter at our efforts to control, we are healed of our deadly seriousness. With the touch of your greasepaint, our faces become transcendent with the radiance of your colors. With the sight of your juggling, we are enraptured by the foolish possibilities of faith. With the sight of your holy saints tripping and falling on their faces, we are freed to fail and then succeed through the mystery of your grace.

READING: THROW OFF THE SHACKLES OF YOUR MINDS

Throw off the shackles of your minds!
Do what you haven't had time to do before.
See what you haven't seen before.
Dream what you haven't let yourself dream before!
Consider the possibilities and laugh a free and hearty laugh!

Laugh at your feeble attempts to make everything come out right.
Laugh at your struggles to understand why the world is the way it is.
Laugh when authorities tell you that their truth is the whole truth,
    because they don't know either.
This is a world where little goes as planned, and what does get done
    often isn't what is needed.
All we can do is laugh at the absurdity of life away from Christ, the
    joking sovereign, our clown ruler of faith.

Let us laugh with our funny God, who dares to believe that in death there is life, and that in caring for our enemies we make friends.

Woe to you who are reluctant to appear foolish, for you are foolish indeed. Woe to you who are afraid to laugh, because God laughs at your sour faces.

In the misery of your days, when everything seems scheduled and unchangeable, remember that you have a choice: a choice to follow the God of time management and profits or the God of foolishness, who loves to smell the roses; a choice to schedule more meetings and be more productive or to sing a few songs from your heart; a choice to organize your free time or to dance a little and see what happens; a choice to be serious or to smile a lot. These are your choices. You can't do both.

If you are too busy to dance, if you are too busy to sing and laugh, then you are too busy for our God, who loves life so much.

Tribes in the American Northwest are convinced that unless worshipers laugh sometime during their sacred ceremonies, the doors will not open to visions and deeper levels of wisdom. For as long as people feel they know God, they are not open to what they do not yet understand. By laughing at their attempts to understand—even at their priests' attempts to explain—the worshipers open up to what is deeper and higher and richer.

HYMN

Sing to the tune of "For All the Saints" (Sine Nomine 10.10.10):

> For all the saints,
> who from their laughter rest,
> for clowns and fools
> the world does not respect.
> We give you thanks,
> O God of merriment.
> Alleluia, alleluia.

MEDITATION

> If we weep, we must also be able to laugh.
> If we despair, we must also be able to rejoice.
> If we bear the burdens of the world, we must still stay light enough to dance.
> For life is good, and the burdens are light if we but smile and know who is our God.
> This is the end of the sermon for today.

(Now make your favorite animal from the Bible using the balloons now being passed out. Give it to someone you don't know and explain why it expresses your faith.)

UNISON PRAYER

O God of bumblers, jugglers, fakes, and saints, we remember your clown-ish people: Saint Philip Neri, who prayed to a funny God; the naked fool who stood alone outside Pskov in the dead of winter and turned away the destruction of Ivan the Terrible; Saint Simeon Salos, who threw nuts at the altar candles to show that candles are not what is important in worship; Saint Francis, who preached your Word to the birds; your holy clowns in the thirteenth century who came out of hidden places to wake parish-ioners when they fell asleep to your Word during services; and your clowns today who go into nursing homes and cheer the lonely and aban-doned, who confront the world's authorities and expose the limits of their wisdom.

When we are too serious, God, send us clowns to teach us how to laugh. When we see only dreary things, send us suspenders and wigs of many colors. And when we are too frivolous, send us your foolish folk to show us that your crazy love is very serious indeed, that it is the salvation of the world.

We thank you, God, for jesters, clowns, and harlequins; for laughter, jokes, and tears; for pathos, penthos, peanuts; we give you thanks and cheer. Hey!

For balloons that make our hearts soar, for soap bubbles that mystify with simple theology, for jugglers' balls and scarves and hoops which somehow defy the forces of reality, we praise your name.

We thank you for jocularity, for words that sound funny like "transub-stantiation," "chthonic," and "kything," because even though words are sometimes not enough, often they are all we have to point us in your direction and to help us describe to others how we feel about you. And we thank you for ourselves, even when we mess up and fall flat on our noses like so many circus clowns.

We thank you for clowns who defy the "reality" of death, who break through the walls that society puts up to separate us from one another, arti-ficial barriers of sex and sexuality, age, race, and nationality. And we thank you for those who are not afraid to laugh, because then we know that your laughter and our work are not yet done. For all this, we give you thanks.

May we see enough to hear and know as little as necessary to realize that all that is, is here now; and that all that can be is now hiding in your foolish dreams. Amen.

HYMN

Sing to the tune "Rise Up, O Men of God!":

> Rise up, O clowns of God!
> Have done with boring things.
> Give heart and mind and soul and strength
> to serve the Fool of kings.
>
> Rise up, O clowns of God!
> The church for you does wait.
> With joy and happiness inside,
> rise up and celebrate.
>
> Rise up, O clowns of God!
> The broken people long.
> Bring in the hope of foolishdom
> and end the night with song.
>
> Lift high the clown in Christ!
> Dance where his clips have clod.
> As foolish lovers of our God,
> rise up and carry on!

Mother's Day

Second Sunday in May

A Litany for Mothers

One: Blessed Mother, we thank you for the wonderful gift of the family, an institution that provides us with support, nurture, and love.

Many: We know a loving family is truly a gift. It is not a gift to be accepted and then put aside, as the servant did who received one talent and buried it in the ground. Rather it is a gift to be opened and developed over the years.

One: We thank you, God, for our mothers, who did much to bring us up with attention and care.

Many: Our mothers helped to teach us right from wrong, comforted us when we were afraid, encouraged us to try new things, and supported us with words and care packages when we left home to start our own lives.

One: Jesus, we acknowledge that you have made us a part of your family.

Many: And this, too, is not a gift to be set aside but a gift that needs to be worked on and developed by getting to know one another as sisters and brothers.

One: Today as we celebrate Mother's Day and give thanks to our mothers, may we also affirm mothers who have careers outside the home, women who have not been able to bear children, women who have adopted, and women who have chosen not to have children of their own yet nurture others. They all have ministries in your name.

Many: Dear God, may we grow in love and understanding as we learn more about our Christian family of sisters and brothers. Although we sometimes seem to be so very different (and in some ways, we are), help us always to feel the bond that unites and supports us in community through your name.

All: We thank you, Mother of us all, for everyone who worries about us as a mother worries and cares for our needs as you do. Amen.

Peace Sunday

Often celebrated in May

A Call to Peace

One: Our leaders proclaim, "Now we have lasting peace!" But there is no peace. There is only a lull in the conflict between people and countries.

Many: God of peace, calm us down when we feel envious of what others have. Otherwise, we deny the good things that you have given us.

One: Expand our sense of national pride, that we may take pride in the people of all nations and cultures.

Many: Calm our fears, that we may reach out to those who frighten and unsettle us with their differences and yet need our help.

One: Take away our desire to engage in battle and destroy the enemy; instead, help us seek to embrace one another as brothers and sisters and to piece together long-term solutions.

Many: Stop us when we erupt in anger and hatred, that we may find a way to tear down the walls that separate us.

One: Bring peace into our unsettled hearts and lives, O God, not that we might be blissful and happy unto ourselves,

Many: But that we might use the peace we feel to calm the turmoil in others. Amen.

Memorial Day

Sunday before May 30

Service: The Costs of War

WORDS OF PREPARATION
This day was created to remember the costs of war.

CALL TO WORSHIP

Today we remember those who died fighting in the military for something they believed in, as well as those who were injured and disabled by the fighting and who carry reminders of this with them.

We remember the pain of separation from loved ones—those who left wondering if they would ever return and those who stayed behind and waited for the dreaded news that loved ones would not be coming home.

We remember those—both combatants and civilians—whose sleep is still haunted by the horrors of warfare.

We remember the resources used to fuel the war machinery.

We remember the industries converted from peaceful purposes into military ones, and the difficulty, costs, and lack of drive to convert them back.

We remember the machinery and supplies left over and left to rust and rot and sink because they could not be used for peaceful means.

We remember the monetary debt built up to fight a war and the economic burden this puts on future generations, diverting economic resources away from providing people's basic needs.

We remember all the physical things that have been destroyed by war and cannot be replaced—wonderful old buildings, people's homes, cities, works of art that expressed the visions of past generations and even cultures.

We remember, too, the cost of seeing war as an option—even as a last and undesired option—for this makes war an easier choice for those who seek easy solutions to complex problems, who value might over right.

We remember the cost of lingering anger toward an enemy who killed loved ones and the hatred that remains in those defeated in war. The hatred left over from World War I contributed to World War II and still continues to fester. Winning the war has not taken care of Nazism, racism, nationalism, or greed.

We remember today those who fought and died to help us see that war solves nothing, but only makes things worse. These are the pacifists. We remember the people of peace from different countries who have heard the call to love our neighbors: Mohandas Gandhi, Leonardo de Vasco, Martin Luther King Jr., Dorothy Day, Francis of Assisi, Brother Roger, and Dorothe Sölle. They felt that if we are willing to live what we believe, to put our bodies on the line for peace, then peace is possible and we will need to study war no more.

We confess our sin of believing, dear God, that threatening violence can make people agree with us. We confess our sin of thinking that war can defeat a people's heart, can make them accept humiliation, can make them agree that we are right. We confess our sin of wanting to believe that the end of a war is the end of the conflict. The end of a war only signals the beginning of the real work of peace, of finding a way to coexist together peacefully. This work was only postponed when the fighting began. Give us the strength not to tire of talking and seeking peaceful means of resolving conflict. Amen.

7

Pentecost

Fifty days after Easter, on the Jewish festival of Pentecost, the Holy Spirit came upon the disciples and followers of Jesus as they were hiding indoors. The account recorded in Acts 2 mentions that flames of fire seemed to appear over the people's heads and they spoke in languages they did not know.

The Jewish Pentecost (Feast of Weeks) is held annually to mark the first fruits of the wheat harvest. The presence of the Holy Spirit signaled that Jesus' spirit could now be with everyone. As Pentecost was the first harvest of the Christian church, this day is known to Christians as the church's birthday. The liturgical color of the day is red, in remembrance of the tongues of fire.

The long season of Pentecost ends when Advent begins and roughly parallels the growing season in the Northern Hemisphere. Fittingly, the liturgical color for the season is green. It is a time for Christians to focus on the Spirit's guidance in their ministries before the liturgical year swings the church's focus back to the birth, life, and death of Jesus. The last Sunday of Pentecost celebrates the sovereignty of Jesus.

The Sunday before Pentecost, when Jesus ascended into heaven, is known as Ascension Sunday. The Sunday after Pentecost is known as Trinity Sunday, commemorating the new Trinity of Father, Son, and Holy Spirit; or Creator, Redeemer, and Sustainer. The three Sundays are celebrated well together.

Pentecost Sunday

Seventh Sunday after Easter

The earliest possible date for Pentecost is May 11 and the latest is June 13. It depends on the date of Easter.

Pentecost Litany: Life into Dust

One: Why, God, did you breathe life into dust? Why did you form us in your image?

Many: We feel like dust so much of the time rather than like anything that is alive. We are tired. Our world looks dreary. Our hope is almost gone.

One: We've built tall towers in an effort to get away from the grit and grime, and to draw closer to you. But we have only succeeded in cutting off the roots to our community.

Many: We've tried to buy the right things, say the right words, and get the right jobs, so that we will feel successful.

One: But something is wrong. Our success feels like a busyness that never ends. We don't know who we are or what we feel anymore. We've lost touch with the dreams of our youth. We spend our nighttime hours spinning plans for tomorrow's work and our daytime hours trying to keep up with demands.

Many: We feel hollow inside, like the dry bones that Ezekiel saw scattered around that valley.

One: We want to breathe of you so deeply, God, that your breath fills our lungs and makes even our fingertips tingle with excitement. We want your Spirit to come again, as it did for Jesus' disciples and followers. Renew our waters of baptism, which have grown brackish. Give our sagging lives the drive to move mountains!

Many: When we finally turn and follow your way, our paper towers begin to fall like stacks of cards, because we are tired of holding them up with dreams undone and lives deferred. With nothing in the way, we again see one another face to face; we see the neglect in our lives. Holding hands, we begin to feel the power of community to move beyond our good intentions.

All: As we talk to one another, the walls that separate us come down. As we tell the stories of our lives, we learn of other truths and different realities. As we share common meals together, as we eat this bread and drink this wine, we invite the Spirit to come into our midst. From dust, O God, you have breathed us into life. O Spirit, inspire us into community. Amen.

Pentecost Day Liturgy: The Day Began

Reader 1:   The day began like most other days. Jews from around the world had gathered in Jerusalem to celebrate the Old Covenant and to worship at the Temple. Jesus' followers were hiding together in one place. Suddenly a sound like the rush of a great wind swept through the room. Upon the head of each of Jesus' followers, there appeared to be flames of fire. Everyone was filled with the Spirit and began to speak in foreign languages. Outside the house, people milling by stopped to listen. Some said:

Group 1:   "We're amazed. They're uneducated and yet they're speaking in foreign languages!"

Reader 1:   Other people said:

Group 2:   "They're just drunk!"

Reader 2:   But Peter spoke up with words from the prophet Joel: "I will pour out my spirit upon all flesh. Your sons and your daughters shall prophesy. The young shall see visions, and the old shall dream dreams" (Acts 2).

Group 1:   Dreams that one day, on the red hills of Georgia, the children of former slaves and the children of former slave owners will be able to sit down together at the communal table.

Group 2:   Dreams that one day every valley shall be exalted, every hill and mountain shall be made low, the glory of God shall be revealed, and all flesh shall see it together.

Reader 2:   God said, "I will pour water on the dry ground and streams on the thirsty land. I will pour my Spirit upon you and your descendants." They shall spring up like rice for a hungry world. God will say, "I am the first and the last. There is no one beside me." They will say, "We are God's."

Reader 1: From that day forth, God's people will speak to everyone on earth, sharing their faith in words, acts, and in their very lives. If not now, then when?

Group 1: We will speak with voices of comfort whenever there is sorrow.

Group 2: We will speak with voices of reconciliation whenever there is anger and hatred.

Group 1: Wherever there is oppression or torture of any kind, we will speak with voices of freedom and justice.

Group 2: Wherever there are people trying to stand up and say, "This is who I am," trying to be heard and understood, trying to be accepted for who they are, we will stand by them and add our own voices of support.

Reader 1: Out of indecisive crowds, we will speak our convictions, for God is doing a new thing!

Reader 2: By ones and twos, we will take a stand to speak with the bold witness of Pentecost, for we are a new people!

Reader 1: If we do not take our stand now, then when?

Reader 2: If we do not speak up today, then why make promises? Promises for tomorrow are as good as none.

Reader 1: We must live our lives now; the moment has arrived.

Reader 2: If not now, then when?

Group 1: Today we will throw open the doors that isolate us from each other and the world. We will raise our voices, dirty our hands, and run the risk of conflict. We will walk forth in the presence of the Spirit, filled to overflowing with life-giving faith.

Group 2: Today we will set out to travel the world with courage, speaking the words the Holy Spirit gives us to speak. We will talk about the hungry and the homeless, about equal pay and equal rights, about taking care of our cultures and our earth. We will speak on the side guided by justice and not on the side ruled by money and power. We will speak as caregivers of every living thing. And we will try not to care what the world will do to us because of our words and our deeds, for we are God's, and there is no other.

All: We will speak with words of justice, with voices of freedom and love!

Reader 1: In places sweltering with the heat of injustice,

Reader 2: In cities sweltering with the heat of oppression,

Group 1: In countries needing to be transformed into oases of freedom,

Group 2: In parched hearts needing the presence of the river of mercy,

All: We will work with deeds of justice, with acts of freedom and love!

Reader 1: We are gathered in this building, and it is the right place to be. We are gathered in this one congregation, and it is the right place to hear the Word of God, to feel the Spirit moving within us, to listen and learn from those gathered here.

Reader 2: We are gathered in this one part of the state, which has many needs, and it is the right place for each of us to be in ministry. We are gathered in this one time, when so much of the world is changing, and we know that dreams long dreamed of can also come true here.

All: We are gathered as individuals, and each of us is in the right place for the Spirit to touch and move within us. The Spirit will give each of us words to speak, words that the thirsty world waits to hear as the dry earth longs for rain.

Reader 1: What needs do you see that require your presence? What words and skills do you have to share with the world right now? I invite each of you to share your words in one sentence. (Each worshiper who is able should stand to speak.)

Reader 2: Let us pray. Great Spirit, you have heard our concerns, and you certainly know our doubts. Give us words and the courage to speak those words each day in our lives. So often we are afraid of showing our faith to others. But when you touch us, we are created anew. Help us realize that we change the world as much by what we choose to do as by what we leave undone. Come to us even as we close ourselves away in our rooms of uncertainty, as we hide in fear. Breathe upon us as Jesus breathed upon his disciples. Offer us new life. Move among us, and move us among all people. We know that out

of our hearts can come living water. As changed people, as
new people in Christ, let us offer this water to a waiting world.
For indeed, if not now, then when?

All: Amen!

Trinity Sunday

First Sunday after Pentecost

Trinity Sunday celebrates the clear emergence of the three main aspects of
God: the Father/Mother, the Son/Child of God, and the Holy Spirit.

Trinity Sunday Litany: In the Beginning

One: In the beginning was God. God was everywhere and in everything. The Alpha and the Omega. In the beginning was the
Word, and the Word was with God, and the Word was God.
In the beginning was the Spirit of God, and the Spirit hovered
over the waters. After the resurrection, Jesus told the disciples
to wait there for the Spirit to come.

Many: Very God of very God, three persons of one substance.

One: Our God is known by many names—Almighty, Protector,
Shepherd, Friend, and Trinity. A three-in-one God, with each
person being equal to the others, yet distinct. God of the past,
the present, and the future. God of the mind, the body, and the
soul. God of the situational, the personal, and the relational.

Many: The Trinity is a way for us to perceive important aspects of
God and to grasp something of the mystery of God.

One: Yahweh: the God of the Old Testament ruled with an iron
hand—omnipotent, omniscient, and omnipresent; the King of
kings, Ruler, Judge, the Unseen who could only be approached
through natural objects, who appeared to Moses in the burning bush.

Many: Jesus: the God of the gospels; the child, a human, who came to
earth and lived among us, who sweated, hungered, and was
tempted; our Savior, Messiah, eternal Word, Prince of Peace,
the promised One. He was sent, crucified, and now is risen.

One: The Holy Spirit: Ruah, the breath of God; the Sophia of the Old Testament; the Pneuma of the New Testament; the spirit of Jesus, unseen but felt; our teacher, counselor, and connection to Jesus.

Many: Creator, Redeemer, Sustainer.

One: God the Creator continues to create through the work of the faithful.

Many: God the Redeemer continues to redeem the brokenness of the world though the healing of the church.

One: God the Sustainer continues to guide as we piece together the mystery of our lives, seeking ways of carrying God's love to others.

Many: Our God is one God, who is and is not the same, one yet three.

One: The one who was, who is, and who is to come.

Many: As the Parent sent the Child, so the Child sent the Spirit to be with us forever.

All: Our God is a God of love who sends us forth to love in many names but in one faith.

Gay/Lesbian Pride Sunday

Last Sunday in June

A Different Liturgy: Minorities

CALL TO WORSHIP

One: We are like odd pieces of old clothing tossed onto a rag pile.

Many: How's that?

One: God goes to that rag pile and gathers together our worn-out, used-up lives, which no one thinks are good for anything more, tears us into strips of cloth, weaves us together, and makes us a quilt.

Many: Our remnants are carefully pieced together, with their frayed threads tucked under and secured. Our worn spots are covered over by the strength of others.

One: What we have in common with one another becomes the pattern of our quilt. Our differences become the brilliant colors.

Many: Our patchwork quilt provides warmth for an often cold world.

One: We are a congregational quilt in process. How are we letting God weave us together?

INVOCATION

O God, we gather together from the hills and the flatlands, from the North and the South, from the East and West. We gather to worship you as we seek your guidance in accepting all your people. We come before you in humility, not understanding the depth of your wisdom. Hear the struggles and joys of our hearts as we pray the prayer Jesus left for all of us:
Pray the Prayer of Our Savior.

PRAYER OF CONFESSION

Dear God of the loom, despite all our words to the contrary and all our efforts to believe that there are real differences among those who claim you, we know that we are all members of your family. We do believe that all who confess Jesus as Savior are true believers; because of this, we are all brothers and sisters.

Yet so often we let our differences get in the way of our beliefs. We respond with fear to what is new or to what we don't understand. We let ourselves think that because people look different, act different, think differently, or feel differently, that they are somehow less than we are and that you care less about them. But you often choose what seems different in order to reveal new dreams. "Behold, I am doing a new thing!" you said about Jesus, an outcast himself. And because those who are seen as different have often suffered because of it, they have come to know how much they need you. Some even take on the burden, as Jonah did, of bearing your message of love back to the people who despise them.

Dear Weaver God, help us come to realize, in what we say and do, that we are all fundamentally the same, and that you weave us together—strength to weakness—that we might be whole. Help our differences become the strength of this congregation as we seek to minister in your name. Amen.

A Different Reading

Reader 1: The church at large tells us that we are different. Yet some of us still linger in the pews and listen to the services, but we do not always worship.

Reader 2: We feel eyes staring at us, and when we glance back, they look quickly away.

Reader 3: We wait by the altar for a few crumbs of support that will keep our hopes alive and nurture our faith during the coming weeks, until we can find a place to call home or until we can return for another moment of sanctuary in the midst of exile.

Reader 4: We wait for an invitation to share who we are, an opportunity to shake hands, exchange smiles, and feel welcome. We are tired of hiding part of ourselves. For those who welcome and affirm us, we give you our heartfelt thanks. Your faith has done much to keep ours alive. There are not many places where God is welcome for those who seem different. The church is not yet a place where all who confess Christ are wanted.

All join in the following chorus:

All:
E   D   C   D   C   D   E
We are your sons and daughters.

C   B   A   A A   G   A   B
We are part of the family of God.

E   D   C   D   C D E
We are your brothers and sisters.

C   B   A   A A G   A   C
We are one in the body of Christ.

Reader 1: We are gay and lesbian. We are African and Asian American. We are Hispanic, European, and American Indian. We possess images and traditions, skills, and compassion that can enrich the church's worship and life.

Reader 2: We have experienced much sadness, yet we still believe. We want to share our stories with you because they are important to us. We want to share them, that we might be understood, certainly. But even more we want to share them so that the part of God that is in us will be revealed.

Reader 3:   Our stories connect us with the wisdom of our past, and they calm our fears. They tell us who we are and ennoble our visions for the future.

Reader 4:   Our stories are sacred to God because they are part of God's story, part of the church's story of bringing freedom and justice to those who are oppressed, those who are persecuted, those who are despised, those who are ignored.
All repeat the chorus.

Reader 1:   Our stories have not often been heard; and when heard, not often accepted; and when accepted, not always included as being part of God's true fabric, part of God's network of sanctioned diversity. Yet the rainbow is a tapestry of many colors.

Reader 2:   The spirit of God is alive within us and needs to be shared if it is to stay alive. If the church will not listen for this spirit in us, will not help enflesh and develop it, if the church will not share the Spirit it has with us, then we must go and live among those who want to hear the good news we bear and want to share the good news that has changed our lives.

Reader 3:   One day we will find a place where we can worship without feeling like visitors, a place where the diversity of believers finds full expression in God.

Reader 4:   One day our searching will stop when we find a home where we can serve God with all that we are, where we can stand up proudly and say "Yes!" without reservation or apprehension.
All repeat the chorus.

Welcoming and Affirming Worship

WORDS OF PREPARATION

On Palm Sunday Jews in Jerusalem were celebrating the Passover and their escape from slavery in Egypt long ago. They were enjoying their affluence and the festivities—the sights, the sounds, and all the wonderful smells of different foods cooking. When Jesus came along at the end of a parade riding on the back of a small donkey, they thought that was funny and they cheered and laid down their cloaks before him. But only the small band of followers recognized that something greater was going on.

Remembering this, we celebrate the arrival of Jesus the Christ in our midst today, especially when he comes in ways we do not expect. May we see what is here for all to see.

CALL TO WORSHIP

Come, all who have been told to stay away from church because of who you are. Jesus' arms are wide enough to embrace you.

Come, all who struggle against injustice and oppression and persecution and have grown weary. Know that God is with you and will not let your efforts be wasted.

Come, all who despair over being rejected by family and friends because you have refused to compromise your God. Rejoice and be glad, for you have shown that your faith is real, that God is not dead but alive, and that God welcomes all people to come.

So come, and worship the God of love, broken for you.

PRAYER

Dear Jesus, you said that it doesn't matter what race we are, or what sex or age or size, whether we are straight or gay, how much money or power we possess, or what physical and mental abilities we may have. But, as was announced on Epiphany, your gospel is for the whole world—not just a select few who were born white, male, and domineering. Your foolish love is for all who confess you as Savior.

We acknowledge before you that we are all sinners and so are equal in your eyes. But, O God, we are under attack. Do not keep silence when those who profess to speak for you use words of anger and hatred! Do not hold your peace during this onslaught! We are suffering under the hands of those who would break us and gnaw on our bones. Speak up! We feel like the psalmist who says, "Strike terror into their hearts! Shoot bolts of your wrath through their dreams. Change their dreams into nightmares, that they may know again who is God!" All we want is to be allowed to worship you in peace and to work out our path of salvation without distraction. O come, dear Jesus, come.

There are many who use their power and money to bend others' lives to do their will instead of yours. Help us to not seek revenge against them; help us rather to produce a softening of their hearts by the suffering of our lives, that your voice may then be heard. Help us draw from our experiences of persecution, that we may bring your compassion in full measure to those who suffer oppression and injustice of any sort.

For the healing of the wounds of the world, for the righting of all injustices, for the renewing of people's lives through your illogical yet transforming love, we ask for your enduring patience, guidance, and wisdom. Amen.

RESPONSIVE READING

One: In all ages there have been people willing to stand up against efforts to limit the gospel.

Many: This is how the Christian church was formed, and the Protestant church.

One: There have always been people willing to stand up against racism, even when some church authorities claimed that God's Word certified nonwhite people as inferior. There have always been people, like Carter Heyward and Harvey Milk, willing to stand up against injustice toward any people.

Many: To all who would say that "those people" are outside the love of God, we say, "That's okay. Come and worship with us. You are our sisters and brothers, and we will not exclude you."

One: To all who would say to us, "Your gospel is too large. We don't want you":

Many: We say, "That's okay, because God does."

One: To those who would say, "We don't need your prophetic gifts":

Many: We say, "We are sorry you feel that way but others do, and we will continue to minister to them for as long as they want us."

One: We will clap and smile, laugh and talk. We will break bread and drink wine together, as we have always done. Our God is God over all creation! And when God looked over what had been created, God saw that all of it was very good!

Many: We are in community with one another, and we will not give up the treasure of our vision. We have a vitality in our diversity that allows us to share the gospel with all people—not just with those who think, look, and act alike.

One: We will take the bones of the gospel to all people and let them enflesh it in their own way.

Many: We will not let any human being bend God's Word in order to keep people in slavery or oppression or injustice.

All: We will be God's faithful people, walking the sometimes lonely road, until this world is transformed by God's love.

MEDITATION

Many of the early translators of the Bible into English were condemned as heretics and were martyred—among them William Tyndale, John Rogers, and Thomas Cranmer. Later translators, such as Elizabeth Cady Stanton, were also criticized and oppressed. Church authorities feared that if laypeople could read the Bible on their own, they would discover the concepts of freedom and justice; no longer would their select group be able to control access to God. On the other hand, when everyone read the Bible, some found (among other matters) that the Bible supported slavery as well as freedom, that it set out rules about what people could and could not eat, that it called for women to be silent in church and for all believers in Christ to be celibate. Only in communities of faith were Christians able to discern Jesus' wisdom in the resulting confusion.

Church politicians have often used this confusion to hide the Word of God behind gossamer veils of human designs. Denominational leaders generally make their decisions in terms of the financial well-being of the institutions they lead. Rarely is serious reflection given to what the Christian faith calls these institutions to do. People's commitments are not based on discerning God's will; they simply want their side to win. Gut feelings become Christian norms, and most arguments end up being rationalizations of those feelings rather than discussions of the implications of faith.

As a result of the church's disregard of theology, laypeople don't know how to talk about their differences of perception in a community of faith. The debate over homosexuality in the church is an example of this. For far too long, the church has not talked about sexuality at all in any form, and now the church is being asked to make decisions without having done its homework.

The church no longer lives on the margins of society, acting as a prophet calling for wholeness; it has taken on the values of society. Only marginalized communities of faith now speak with prophetic voices, with visions of insight. Marginalized communities live a type of heroism that looks like weakness. They are humble, loving, and peaceful. They struggle against society's envy, greed, lust, and thirst for power.

Jesus cut through all the religious rules and said that there were just two commandments that mattered: to love God with your whole life, and to love others as you love yourself. Then, to show the disciples what this love required, Jesus tied a towel around himself and washed their feet. "This," he said, "is what I call you to do."

CONFESSIONAL PRAYER: STATIONS OF THE CROSS

O God, there is so much that is wrong in the world! So much hatred and anger and jealousy and envy and greed, and we are a part of it! Please hear our prayers as we follow the stations of the cross, accompanying Jesus on his journey to Calvary.

One: We take what we want from the earth, from our institutions, and from one another so that we may be more comfortable, more secure, and more powerful.

Many: Forgive our greed, dear Jesus.

One: We say nuclear power is good because it's cost-effective, but we let future generations worry about what to do with radioactive waste.

Many: Forgive our desire for cheap comfort, dear Jesus.

One: We say it's acceptable to pollute the air because the trees will clean it up, but then we cut down the rain forests.

Many: Forgive our lack of caring, dear Jesus.

One: We say people with AIDS are being judged by God, but we consider people with cancer to be unlucky.

Many: Forgive our prejudice, dear Jesus.

One: We say it's harmless to kill off animal species because there are plenty of others around, and we forget that all of nature is interconnected.

Many: Forgive our cavalier attitude, dear Jesus.

One: We say we have a right to oppress people if they look, smell, or act different, because this is our town and we can run it the way we want.

Many: Forgive our haughtiness, dear Jesus.

One:	We say we believe in Jesus and feel his pain on the cross, but whenever a ministry reaches out to a despised group, we either are first in line to persecute the upstarts or we stand around and do nothing to help.
Many:	Forgive our fearfulness, dear Jesus.
One:	We say physical and verbal abuse are justified when done in the name of love, but the ends do not make the means ethical.
Many:	Forgive our rationalizations, dear Jesus.
One:	We say we can ignore global climatic changes because we control nature, but we are part of the earth and to the earth we will return.
Many:	Forgive our detachment, dear Jesus.
One:	We say we can react in any way we want when we're afraid, and this can include acts of massive destruction, but Jesus calls us to let go of our fears and follow him.
Many:	Forgive our weariness when conflicts are not quickly resolved, dear Jesus.
One:	We say we don't have to recycle because there are plenty of resources, but we forget that most of the world has little access to them.
Many:	Forgive our throwaway society, dear Jesus.
One:	We say feelings aren't as important as thoughts, and therefore we downplay the feminine within us. We also undervalue the thoughts of women.
Many:	Forgive us when we create throwaway people, dear Jesus.
One:	We say those who have no homes or jobs or food have brought their troubles upon themselves, but we forget that many "successful" people were born into the affluence and privilege they enjoy.
Many:	Forgive our self-centeredness, dear Jesus.
One:	We confess, O God who lives among the abandoned, the forsaken, and the poor, that too often we have taken for granted what we have and bemoaned what we do not have, forgetting that all we need is faith in you.
Many:	Forgive us for wanting faith only for our own gain, dear Jesus. O God, we ask you to strip us of everything but our faith so

that nothing gets in the way of following you on your pilgrimage. Make thoughts of you always dwell in our hearts and in our minds, and feelings of you always inspire us to seek out new ways of caring for your world. May we see, in everyone we meet, your Jesus. Amen.

GOOD NEWS BENEDICTION

One: We have been to the hissing assemblies
that hide God behind spurious debates,
where large Bibles are pounded with pietistic fervor
to support fear,
where hollow poses reveal calculated diversions.

But faith can be held under water only so long
before it surges to the surface and,
with a mighty cry of freedom, shouts:

Many: "I am alive, and so is my God who loves the world!"

One: And once more God is felt in lives reborn in careful thought,
in heartfelt acts of compassion that endear and endure,
where common deeds compel others to leave the dry tombs
where no one sleeps anymore,
and come to the baptismal waters with longing and hope.

The handful of grass that we hold high on the hillside
where we sup and commune in small groups,
is a temple dearer to God than the mighty sanctuaries
that hold thousands of people frozen in sacred banality,
where power is praised and money worshiped,
and mealy-mouthed ministers mumble of all you can get
if you take up their offer right now.

Many: Our temple, though humble, embraces the world.

One: Now, with the touch of this dawn upon our face,
we are renewed within.
We feel the resurgent drive to share simple words,
to welcome and affirm,

to head out on the road again
to wherever it leads, to share and pray
with care, and say:

Many: "Our God loves the world!"

U.S. Independence Day

Sunday before July 4

Prayers for Religious Freedom

INVOCATION
Dear God, come, be among us. Send your Spirit as we gather in your name. We thank you for the freedom we have to believe as we will. We are grateful for those who have worked hard to establish and preserve this gift. Help us use this freedom not to go our own ways but to seek out opportunities to talk to one another and deepen our communal understanding of you and your ways.

Live among us as we seek to be responsible to the requirements of our faith: to go to those who need the good news we bear. Be with us now as we pray with the words that Jesus taught his community of believers.

Pray the Prayer of Our Savior.

PRAYER OF CONFESSION
God of freedom, we are thankful for those who have fought hard for religious freedom. We thank you also for the responsibilities that this freedom brings. It challenges us to deepen our faith. It challenges us to seize opportunities to share our beliefs with one another and to share your message with those who are in need. These challenges are especially important in a time when movies glorify violence, people are killed over minor disagreements, and a large part of our society lives without hope.

We realize we need to go to the abusers as well as to the abused, but it is hard not to judge and take sides. We need to sit with the oppressors as well as with those being oppressed, because both sides need the guidance of your Word. We need to take mercy into places where the rule of law falls short of justice, and to take compassion where the rights of some fail to correct the wrongs done to others.

We thank you for giving us faith—not that we might save ourselves, but that we might save others along with ourselves. We feel your Spirit at work in this congregation. In our freedom, O God, let us not forget to live out the disciplines of faith. Amen.

Transfiguration

August 6

The Transfiguration commemorates the occasion when Jesus took Peter, James, and John to a mountaintop to pray. While there, the three disciples watched Jesus become radiant as he talked with Moses and Elijah. Theologically, Moses represented the Jewish law and Elijah was to reappear just before the Messiah arrived. Jesus, in this situation, is viewed as the fulfillment of the law and as the Messiah who was to come.

Catholics and Episcopalians observe the Transfiguration on August 6, but other denominations commemorate this event on the Sunday before Ash Wednesday. For other liturgics, see chapter 4.

A Litany for the Transfiguration: Today We Remember

RESPONSIVE READING

One: Today we remember both the nuclear bombing of Hiroshima and the Transfiguration of Jesus.

Many: What do they have to do with each other?

One: Both of them speak to us of light—light almost intolerable, light almost beyond human understanding. Hiroshima suggests not just the light of the atomic bomb, but also the light that this event shed on our inability to secure lasting peace through conventional means.

Many: So what are you saying?

One: The light of Jesus' Transfiguration, when he stood illumined with Moses and Elijah, reveals to us that we live by faith and that what we do must come out of our faith.

Many: So that God's light shines through what we do?

One: And our faith is evident to all who see us.

Inscriptions of Hiroshima

One: Upon our hearts God has inscribed Jesus' name.

Many: Upon the cornerstones of our buildings and on the doorways over our entrances we have inscribed the visions of our hearts.

One: We have sown the seeds of our faith upon the winds and brought hope and compassion to suffering people.

One: We have also sown the seeds of our doubt upon the winds and contaminated the earth with our prejudices and fears.

One: We remember today Hiroshima and Nagasaki, where atomic bombs inflicted horrible suffering upon hundreds of thousands of civilians and ended our dream of using science and technology to achieve lasting peace.

Many: We confess that, at times, the rhetoric of war and the desire for its spoils have overcome our resolve for peaceful resolution. We have marked foreign lands with the blinding inscriptions of fire and radiation sickness.

One: Yet there is redemption. The spring winds from the east awaken new dreams within us. The summer winds from the south warm the earth and heal our wounds. The fall winds from the west cool our passions and mature our thoughts. And the winter winds from the north bring solitude and a sifting of hopes and unfulfilled desires.

All: Dear God of the Hibakusha, we are a people numbed by the ease of war, lured by the simplicity of dropping an atomic bomb on a city when we can't resolve a conflict. We need to be reminded that we are all family. We need to have Christ be the good news in our lives again. Help us live out the dreams we inscribe in words over the doorways of our buildings. As the winds of struggle blow across our world, inscribe our eyes with your vision, our minds with your wisdom, our hearts with your compassion, and our hands with your mercy. Help us sow the seeds of faith so that those coming after us may harvest peace. Amen.

Human Rights Sunday

A Sunday in early August

Litany: Drums of Witness

One: During this week in history, much has happened. In 1943, Franz Jagerstatter was executed by the Nazis for refusing to serve in the German army. In 1945, the cities of Hiroshima and Nagasaki were destroyed by atomic bombs. In 1965, the Voting Rights Act for African Americans was signed into law. This week also marks the beginning of intertribal ceremonies for American Indians.

All: *Selah!*

One: Franz Jagerstatter stepped forward for the rights of conscientious objectors.

Many: The survivors of Hiroshima and Nagasaki stand up and call us to see the inhumanity and insanity of nuclear weapons.

One: Americans sat down and refused to move until African Americans could vote without interference.

Many: American Indians gather to affirm the goodness of their traditions in the land of their ancestors.

All: *Selah!*

One: There have always been persons who do not look away from suffering but stand beside those who are in pain, whose rights and lives are being taken away. They are not afraid to speak up and name the injustice, preach against the prejudice, challenge the lies, and proclaim that indeed God's love is greater than any hatred and more powerful than any fear. They are quiet people who stand in front of the madness and say "Enough!" They are caring people who go to places of harm and comfort the abused, strong people who confront businesses planning new ways of dismantling the sanctity of life and say "This is wrong." These people have been willing to sacrifice their careers, their dreams, and their lives in order to help others and be true to their beliefs. The suffering they endure because of their witness does not mark them with the rancor of bitterness and anger; it transfigures them with God's light.

All: *Selah!*

One: The beat of Jagerstatter's heart sounded out the faith of a man in love with the gospel of peace.

Many: The solitary six-count drumbeat of the members of the Japanese Lotus Sutra, who stand quietly in the rain witnessing to peace, remind us of our part in the madness of nuclear war and greed.

One: The drums of African Americans invite us to celebrate life even when life isn't all that we want it to be. They invite us to dance with joy to the deep rhythms of life even when the heaviness of concerns weigh us down.

Many: The drums of American Indians call us to reclaim our customs and traditions as sources of wisdom, to listen again for the guidance of the Great Spirit.

All: *Selah!*

One: Before us have gone ordinary people of simple courage; people we call our teachers, pastors, prophets, and martyrs. People who stepped forward and did what was right, even if it meant persecution, because they could do no less. People who sat down on buses and stood up in front of police dogs and refused to cooperate with evil. People who opened the doors of opportunity and equality and were criticized and chastised because of their actions. Blessed are they who have fought injustice with deeds of love!

Many: We are the offspring of this witness, inheritors of this noble vision and courageous faith, this reckless love that marks a trail through the desert of conflicting opinions and self-centered values. May we be found as worthy when our days are done.

All: *Selah!*

Labor Day (Workers' Sunday)

Sunday before the first Monday in September

Liturgics for Workers' Sunday

PREPARATION

Labor Day was created by labor unions to honor workers. Today we remember those who work for a living and those who struggle for equal rights for all workers.

CALL TO WORSHIP

> Come, all of you who work two or more jobs to pay the bills,
> who live in fear of being laid off,
> who seek meaningful work,
> who are underemployed and seek work that uses more of your
>   skills,
> who constantly have to work overtime just to keep your job,
> who have to do some tasks you don't think are ethical,
> who work full time and still can't afford any luxuries that society
>   says are important,
> who are immigrants and migrants and can find only menial or
>   seasonal work,
> who are stuck in boring careers and feel time and dreams slipping
>   away.
> God hears your cries.

We remember those who have worked, and sometimes died, to secure the workers' rights to a living wage and decent benefits; rights to a work environment safe from pesticides and chemicals, nuclear radiation, power machinery, and materials that cause black lung and brown lung. We remember those who have fought against sweatshops and against child labor.

In the struggle for all to have enough food, shelter, and clothing, we acknowledge that it is the poor who suffer the most. Today we remember those who work and are heavy laden. To you Jesus says, "Come."

Homecoming Sunday

Generally a Sunday in September

Homecoming Sunday focuses on the congregation reuniting after summer vacations. It represents a regathering and a revisioning of plans and ministries.

A Liturgy: Weaving

WORDS OF MEDITATION

Weaver of the threads of life, pull us together into your blanket of love. Warm the world with the work from your loom through the work of our hands. Brighten drab lives with your colors and designs, excite us with the variety of textures of your people. Weave us into your new creation.

PROCESSIONAL

Sing "Raise Your Voices in Praise," by Ken Medema.

CALL TO WORSHIP

One: Dear God of the odd, who calls those who seem out of place in this world: the different, the weird, the strange; the wanderer, the visitor, the outsider; the marginalized, disenfranchised, and institutionalized,

Many: Help us extend your invitation to all people to come, to worship, and to be part of your community of faith. Enable us to accept that your church is not made from whole seamless cloth but is pieced together from flawed and frayed remnants into a warm comforter.

One: We are not a strong people, a superior people, or even a particularly talented people.

Many: We are a bunch of ragged, used-up, worn-down, torn-up misfits who can't seem to make our lives work on our own. And we don't want to be on our own. We want to rely only on your help and guidance. We want to be a humble, faith-filled people who somehow make things happen.

One: Give us the strength to remain different and allow you to weave our differences into the pattern of your blanket. We ask that we may always be an odd people, made holy by your presence in whatever we say and do.

Many: Help us heed your call to welcome the stranger and the friend, to comfort and console, to encourage and enable as your presence in us bursts forth in a rainbow of ministries. Help us reach into the world with threads of your love, that others may become new patterns in your *serape*.

ANTHEM

Sing "It's More Than You. It Is More than Me," by Henry Krieger.
The pastor delivers a sermon.

PRAYER OF COMMITMENT

Weaver of all creation, we can imagine you sitting with a loom in an open shed or a bare room, carding and spinning wool, carefully selecting yarns of different colors and textures, and, in the quiet of the day, weaving them into a blanket begun a long time ago. We can hear the rustle of the shuttle as you slide it between the warp yarn, and the soft thump of the batten as you compact the weft into the weave. The sounds of the weaving and the feeling of this place bring us peace.

Weaver God, card us to remove impurities. Spin our insecurities into assurances of you. Weave us so closely together that we learn to rely on one another when our own strength fails, that we may endure together in the task of comforting and challenging the world. May the variety of textures to your people—the coarse and the smooth, those with lumps and imperfections—excite us with so many possibilities for ministry that we will not want to pull out what we don't like or understand, and thus unravel the whole blanket. Help the many hues of our lives together—the indigos and ochres, the emeralds and magentas—brighten the lives and dreams of others that have been dulled with worry, pain, and doubt. Weave us all into a tapestry of your new creation.

May what we have spoken of here move into our hearts and come to be.

HYMN OF COMMITMENT

Sing "Take My Life and Let It Be," by Frances Havergal.

CLOSING HYMN

Sing "Weave," by Rosemary Crow.

Christian Education Sunday

For the start of the Sunday-school year in September

Christian Education Sunday is a way of getting more people involved. It can also be observed at the end of the school year as a way of thanking the teachers and celebrating the graduates.

A Service for Christian Education Sunday: God of Wisdom

CALL TO WORSHIP

Kything Spirit, who makes known all the depths of God, God of wisdom, counsel, and understanding, from you comes everything we have. We praise you and thank you for sharing your love.

Dear Christ Jesus, Light of the world, Teacher of God, incarnate Word and eternal Truth, we thank you for coming to be a light for those sitting in shadows. We thank you for inviting us to be among your students.

Dear Holy Spirit, our Helper and our Strength, we praise you for revealing the essential things of God. We thank you for dividing your gifts among all people, so that only in community with one another can we experience the fullness of God. We are grateful to you for leading us along the path of wisdom.

PRAYER

Gracious God, who would have all people come to a knowledge of you, we remember before you, on this special day, every public educational enterprise established for our instruction and care: the elementary, middle, and high schools, the colleges and universities, the seminaries and trade schools, the extension and night schools. Enlighten and inspire all who teach in them with wisdom, sensitivity, and justice. Give to the trustees and administrators the vision and courage to see beyond today's problems and budgets to the needs of the future. Should any of them become discouraged or distracted, comfort, guide, and strengthen them.

O God, please be attentive to the educational work of the church. Guide parents to instruct their children in the particulars of faith through their words and actions. Through the Holy Spirit, touch the minds and lives of our pastors and teachers, so that they may lead us into the knowledge that can make us wise of heart and daring in ministry.

Be mindful also, O God, of our students of all ages. Arouse us to diligence in study. Fill us with the spirit of honor and reverence for those who have gone before us and those of other traditions who also seek to learn truth. Preserve us in honesty and in the seeking of wisdom. Keep us pure of mind, strong in body, and within the balance of community.

Guide us in the study of the Scriptures, in the listening of prayer, in the guidance of nature, and in the pursuit of truth, wherever it is found, in all our thoughts, words, and deeds.

May the example of Jesus in his childhood and youth, in his careful study as an adult, in his unselfish service and openness to all people, in his example in life and death, be our constant inspiration. Hear us, gracious God. Amen.

Worldwide Communion Sunday

First Sunday in October
Worldwide Communion Sunday focuses on the unity that all Christians share.

Time to Repair: An Ecumenical Service for Saint Francis of Assisi

WORDS OF PREPARATION

In 1986, 160 representatives from religions around the world gathered in the Italian town of Assisi to pray in tribute to the spirit of Saint Francis. The Buddhists chanted, Zoroastrians lit fires, American Indians danced, and the Archbishop of Canterbury prayed. For a day, much of the fighting around the world paused in tribute to the simple man of peace. Hindus shared with Jains, Shintoists played bamboo flutes, Muslims met with African animists, and Mother Teresa talked with Archbishop Methodios of the Orthodox Church.

PRELUDE AND PROCESSIONAL
The following hymn is sung to a Bob Marley reggae tune.

(refrain)
> I don't want to be without Jesus in my life.
> I don't want to be without Jesus in my life.

> I can hear the birds singing,
> I can see the ocean blue,
> I can taste the mango sweetly,
> I can feel the evening's cool, that's why . . .

(refrain)

> There is just no reason without
> the season of God's joy.
> There is just no meaning without
> the leading of our God, that's why . . .

(refrain)

> With all of creation singing
> I need to dance.
> Whenever I feel uncertain
> I always chant this tune, that's why . . .

(refrain)

CALL TO WORSHIP
We gather today to celebrate the unity in God that all Christians share. We also celebrate Saint Francis of Assisi, whose feast day is October 3. Francis lived in the twelfth century. Like other young people, he grew up planning what he was going to get out of life. When the realities of war shattered his illusions, he began seeking answers elsewhere. One day he heard God asking him to "repair my church." At first, Francis thought this meant to repair the abandoned chapel of San Damiano; but while he was busy putting the walls back together, he realized that it was the church's faith that God had asked him to rebuild. Francis began to give away his possessions so that he could see and follow God as closely as possible. People were attracted by this simple faith and began to gather

around him. Francis and his followers breathed new life into the church of his day and rebuilt its spiritual life.

RESPONSIVE READING: TIME TO REPAIR

One: Brothers and sisters, it is time again to repair the church.

Many: This does not mean we must repair the buildings made of wood and stone, but rather the church that lives inside us.

One: We share a simple vision of great worth. Over the centuries, we've constructed rituals and formulas of words to protect and preserve this treasure. But rituals lose the poignancy of their symbolism, words change their meanings, and often we are uncertain about which way to turn when technology raises questions that have never been asked.

Many: Let us return to a simple faith in which we speak about God in the words that are in our hearts and we express our faith through the experiences of our lives.

One: We think there are many differences between Congregationalists and Baptists, Methodists and Episcopalians. We feel there are even greater differences between Protestants and Roman Catholics, between the Greek and Russian Orthodox. But these differences are not important, because we all seek the same God.

Many: There are as many differences within this congregation as there are among denominations, yet we all worship together.

One: We rebuild the church not by tearing down hollow structures that have lost their meaning. We rebuild by starting with the foundation of our faith.

Many: We rebuild by listening for God's voice in our lives.

One: We rebuild by setting aside what distracts us from following God more closely.

Many: We rebuild by humbling ourselves so that we live without pretense, without illusion, without any need to make something of ourselves; for we serve God, not ourselves.

One: We rebuild by sharing our struggles with one another and by listening for God's message in others' words. By learning from one another, we strengthen the community of faith.

Many: We rebuild by welcoming those marginalized by poverty, illness, or wealth.

Many: Saint Francis calls us to live a simple life, to celebrate the goodness of all creation;

Many: To sing with the songs of the birds, dance with the trees in the wind, and dream with the movement of the stars.

PRAYER

One: Personal God, you live all around us. Holy is your name.

Many: May your world come and your will be done on earth.

One: Give us today the things we need, and forgive us when we turn away from you.

Many: Help us forgive those who hurt us.

One: Help us not to be led away by temptation but to be delivered from questionable activities.

Many: For yours is the way of life we desire, the power to make it happen, and the wisdom that lasts forever.

All: Amen.

UNISON PRAYER

Religion sometimes gets in the way of our faith, O God of all creation. We confess that we hide behind church forms for assurance when we are confused, that we too often let Sunday worship take the place of our faith. Instead of praying each day on our own, we rely on the church's prayers on Sunday. Instead of dealing with the responsibilities our participation in communion gives us, we let the Sunday worship service be the extent of our ministry. Instead of leaving here to share the good news with the world, we let our pastors shoulder this responsibility. We have become like hollow buildings, well designed and beautiful but empty inside. Each new problem that drops into our lives echoes the depth of our loneliness.

Help us, O God, to feel again your movement in our lives. Help us share again with others and see again what your hope means to them. Help us always to live faithfully and simply, that nothing may get in the way of serving you. Help us always to love one another, that our differences will not build up new walls of separation. Help us celebrate the sacredness of every living thing and the presence of your Spirit in every single person, that we may be a true and enduring community. Amen.

BENEDICTION

Saint Francis has shown us how to live. Let us go from here seeking God in all that we do and speaking of God in all that we say. Sisters and brothers, let us rebuild God's church, and let us begin today.

Reformation Sunday

Sunday before October 31

Reformation Sunday focuses on the Reformation which Martin Luther began when he nailed the ninety-five theses to the door of Wittenberg Church. The central concept is of the priesthood of all believers with direct access to God.

A Reformation Sunday Service: The Priesthood of All

One: We believe in the priesthood of all believers.

Many: We believe that each of us has been called to share God with the world, even though we may feel unworthy of such a responsibility.

One: We believe that we are justified by faith alone and not by anything we can do.

Many: We believe, though, that without good works our faith is hollow.

One: We come knowing that we can share anything with God and God will listen.

Many: We come knowing that we can celebrate who we are and dream of what we can become.

One: We come together to share in community, to serve one another the bread and the wine.

Many: We come together not to fulfill any Sunday obligation or to revel in the magic of ritual. We come together to worship God and to learn from one another more about following God.

One: Let us then worship and learn.

READING: IN THE MIDDLE AGES

In the Middle Ages, the concerns of this world were merely for survival. The church was a formal structure that offered up transitory magic instead of eternal mystery, substituted hollow rituals and heavy obligations for a living faith, and matched future rewards in heaven to how well one endured the hardness of this life. It was a pretty show with smells and bells, but offered people little when the magic failed.

Then in England in the 1300s, John Wyclif said "Let's translate the Bible into English so that everyone can read it. There's important stuff in there!" The church authorities (who could read the Bible's Latin) either didn't like the idea of sharing their power or didn't care for Scripture being referred to as "stuff," but they simply said "No!" After Wyclif died, the church hid his body. His handful of followers, however, continued his work.

In Czechoslovakia in the 1400s, Jan Hus agreed with Wyclif about the Bible, but he believed that more needed to be done: Church services should also be in the language of the people, so that they could understand what was going on. Laypeople should receive the wine of communion, because they were at least as Christian as the clergy. The church authorities, who liked the God-ordained scheme they had worked out on their own, didn't like Hus and burned him at the stake. But the number of his followers had grown so large that Hus's minority party became the majority in Czechoslovakia, and the resulting Bohemian Church brought in the reforms anyway.

In Germany in the 1500s, Martin Luther agreed with Wyclif and Hus but said that neither one went far enough. So on October 31, 1519, he nailed to the door of Wittenberg Chapel a list of ninety-five points of disagreement with the Catholic Church. He felt the church had grown distant from people, that the church's elaborate rites and rituals kept people from God, and that the simplicity and directness of Jesus and the early disciples had been lost. The church had changed from being a community to being an institution. By now, the number of reformed-minded protesters had grown so great that the Catholic Church was thrown out of Germany and the Protestant Reformation began on a large scale.

In the 1600s, the Catholic Church began a Counter-Reformation to try to get its land and power back, but that's getting ahead of the story.

Suddenly, the doors to the church were opened wide; people streamed in, and people streamed out. Laypeople were invited in to share the administration of the church—its theology, worship, and pastoral care. And all Christians were invited to go out into the world and share the good news with others.

No longer was the message of the church only for people's souls, as if the life of this world didn't matter. The Protestant Church cared about people's minds and bodies as well. The church took notice of where people lived, how they talked, what they ate, the kind of work they did. Luther borrowed barroom tunes, put new words to them, and made them hymns. Church authorities were outraged, but the people loved them and came back to church with renewed vigor because finally there was something for them. They took their newfound faith into the streets and their homes, into the fields and mountain hamlets. A revolution swept first through Europe and then through the world. Because it was now okay to think, science and the arts flourished and brought in the Age of Enlightenment. The feudal system, which had locked the poor into eternal poverty, was broken. Equal rights for all people began to be a concern. People were whole again.

As Protestants, we are inheritors of this faith. We believe in the priesthood of all believers, whereby each of us can talk directly with God and each of us can take Jesus directly to others.

Yet today, society again says that the church should only concern itself with people's souls; that religion, at most, should take up only a corner of people's lives. The church has largely accepted this role. Laypeople again let church professionals do most of the spiritual work, and we live the greater part of our lives in servitude to some job.

What we have gained is a tradition in which all who are called to faith are also called to witness to that faith in God's name. What we have lost is our zest to share. Is it time for a new reformation? The church again is supporting the status quo; it no longer comprises the revolutionary band of followers it once did. The emptiness of our material society is pushing many people to seek meaning and spirituality in life. The church largely has forgotten the answers, because it has forgotten how to nourish community. Instead of offering magic like the fifteenth-century church, today's church offers the benefits of an elixir: take it once a week, and you'll be fine until next Sunday.

PRAYER

O God of the Reformation, you are not a God for only part of our lives, and the church is not a place only concerned with our souls. Everything we are belongs to you, and everything we say and do can be part of preparing your way.

Re-form our hearts into something that affirms the goodness of all creation—of body, mind, and soul—for only by experiencing you through all three can we see you completely. You did not give us bodies solely for toil, labor, and sweat, but also to enjoy pleasures. You did not give us minds only to make plans, but also to create. You did not give us souls only to long for a future of living eternally with you, but also to dream and find ways of living with you now.

Please remove, O God, whatever prevents us from approaching you. Embolden our courage to overcome whatever prevents us from going out with your name to others. May we be like John Wyclif, Jan Hus, and Martin Luther. When something holds back your Spirit, let us say stand up and say, "What gives?" Help us nail signs on our doors that proclaim, "This is what we are about. Here we will stand, because we can do nothing else. This is what we believe and who we are."

Relight the fire within our hearts, that we may be warmed and that others may see your glow. Give us good beer and hearty bread for our bellies, lusty singing and joyous dancing for our souls, for we are not a dour people with nothing to offer a tired world. Our God is the God of creation, with comfort, laughter, and joy for all who need a place to rest and a place to call home. Amen!

All Saints' and All Souls' Days

Sunday before November 1 and 2

All Saints' and All Souls' days commemorate the great leaders of the past and call to mind the faithful who have died over the last year.

A Service for All Saints' and All Souls' Days: A Great Number

Call to Worship

We remember today those of the faith who have stood strong and gone on before us. May we not be found wanting when our final day comes.

Hymn

Sing the following words to the tune of "Glory to God, Whose Witness-Train" (Bedford):

> All praise to God, whose Spirit guides
> our teachers of the faith,
> who fear not poverty or death,
> all for God's touch of grace.
>
> Almighty God, you seek to reach,
> through our imperfect ways,
> to smooth a brow, to feed and clothe,
> to heal, all in your place.
>
> Jesus, your Spirit lives in us,
> with its inviting light.
> Help us confront the angry world
> and ease the restless night.

All who can stand should do so.

Reader 1: Look! A great number of people, which no one can count, from every nation and tribe, out of every city and village, people of all languages and cultures, are standing before the throne of God, dressed in flowing robes and waving palms in their hands.

Many: They are shouting with a great voice: "Our salvation is in God, who sits on the throne; in Jesus Christ, the One who died for us; and in the Spirit, who leads us home!"

Reader 2: The world has not known what to do with them: the faithful. They have seemed too naive, too impractical, and too idealistic. Their ways have not been the ways of the world. They have stood up and spoken from pulpit and pew to remind us of God's way. They have wandered in deserts and through forests, along city streets and over farmlands. They have lived in parsonages and huts, on heating grates and smelly trash dumps, that they might minister to others. Some were ignored or thrown into prison for speaking God's words, and they were tempted to compromise their faith. Others were tortured, murdered, and left by the roadside as a warning to others who might want to follow God's way of love. They have believed the words of Psalm 139, that there was no place that they could go that God's love would not go with them.

Many: They were killed by the machete and the gun, by bombs and napalm. Poverty, ill health, and starvation, even our own indifference and sometimes hostility to their message could not convince them to give up. These are the ones—the company of the committed, those who endured hardship and death—who now stand before God, washed, with clean hair, and with hope in God for justice and mercy for those who oppress the poor.

Reader 1: This community of the faithful hunger and thirst no more. Their memories of suffering fade as God heals their wounds with living water, as God wipes away every tear from their eyes.

HYMN

Sing "For All the Saints, Who from Their Labors Rest" (Sarum).
All those who can kneel should do so.

Reader 2: Let us pray: God of inspiration, our Creator, who gave us talents to use, we offer you our heartfelt thanks and praise for the holy lives of your servants—the prophets, martyrs, and saints of all ages and sexes who have shone as lights in the world, who dedicated and sacrificed their lives in your service. We thank you for the great community we have with them. In your presence, we remember those who never gave up trusting in you:

The congregation is asked to mention the names of those who have guided them and are now dead.

Reader 1: May this great cloud of witnesses be an inspiration to us when we falter. May we learn to run the race that is set before us, always looking to God, the Creator, Redeemer, and Sustainer of our faith. May we be found worthy to join this glorious company when our time on earth is done. Amen.

All who can stand should do so.

HYMN

Sing "Apostles, Prophets, Martyrs" (Lancashire).

>Our teachers, prophets, martyrs,
>and all who lived for you,
>who sang the song of living
>while suffering for your Word,
>for those who went before us,
>for those who suffer now,
>may we be strong in witness
>and fill baptismal vows.

Reader 2: Blessed are those who are persecuted because they look out for the needs of others, for they live in the presence of God.

Many: If we choose, who can separate us from the love of God? Can poverty, hardship, lack of prestige, persecution, or even torture stop us from serving God?

Reader 1: No! All these things are but chaff in the wind. Not even death can persuade us to turn away. For if God is with us, what do we have to fear?

Many: So says the Amen, the Alpha, and the Omega, the eternal Word, the faithful and true Witness, who was dead and is alive again: "Be faithful, even unto death, and I will always be with you."

Reader 2: To Jesus who loves us, to the Spirit who empowers us, to God our Father and Mother who holds us close, be glory and dominion, dreams and visions, forever and ever. Amen.

HYMN
Sing "Ten Thousand Times Ten Thousand" (Eastham).

Thanksgiving Sunday

Sunday before the fourth Thursday in November

A Eucharistic Service: Great Thanksgiving

One: May God live in our hearts!

Many: May God be present in our words and in the movements of
our hands!

One: Thanks be to God for the gift of life!

Many: It brings us much joy to thank our God, the Creator of heaven
and earth!

One: God, you created all that is, bringing light out of the shadows
and giving us darkness in which to rest and draw closer to
you. You made the rolling hills and the flowing rivers, the animals that run and the birds that soar. You created us with your
Spirit out of the soil of the earth. When we turned away from
you to pursue our own pleasures and failed to love other
people, you still continued to love us and tried to guide us.
When we were taken prisoner by other nations because of our
selfishness, you went with us and brought us back from our
captivity. In the midst of our indecision about what god to
serve, you came to us and made a covenant with us: if we
would follow only you, then you would be our God. When we
went too far in our own schemes of grandeur and wealth, your
prophets and teachers reminded us of your ways. Then
because we continued to fall short, you sent your Child, your
dear Jesus, to be our Savior. As the heavens sang of your glory,
on that night long ago, so we join their celebrations.

Many: As Mary and Joseph went from Galilee to Judea and found no
place to sleep, so Jesus would later go from Nazareth to
Jerusalem and find no place where he was accepted.

One: As in simplicity Jesus was born, as in rejection and misunderstanding he lived, and as in the humiliation of his death, so in communion with his suffering and his resurrection you gave birth to your church. Deliver us from slavery to matters that lead us nowhere and only drain your love from our hearts. Make a new covenant with us.

Many: As your Word became flesh and dwelt among us, as a woman gave herself up to bring life into the world, so on the night in which Jesus gave himself up for us, he took bread, gave thanks to you, broke the bread, gave it to his disciples, and said: "Take, eat; this is my body which is broken for you. Do this in remembrance of me."

The bread is shared.

When the meal was over, he took a cup from the table, gave thanks and said: "Drink from this, all of you; this is my blood of the new covenant, poured out for you and for many for the forgiveness of sins. Do this, as often as you drink it, in remembrance of me" (Luke 22).

The wine or juice is shared.

In remembrance of these simple yet profound acts of Jesus the Christ, we offer our lives in thanksgiving. As Jesus then got up, tied a towel around himself and washed the feet of the disciples, so we are called to be people willing to suffer in order to bring healing and comfort to those who are in need: the hungry, the homeless, the poor, the ill, those in hospitals, prisons, and hospices. We proclaim the mystery of faith through the witness of our actions.

Christ has died,
Christ is risen,
Christ will come again.

Dear God, pour out your Holy Spirit upon us. We wait for you. Be in this bread and juice. Move within us, that we may be for the world the body of Christ.

Through your Spirit make us one with Christ, one with one another, and one in our ministries to all the world. Give us strength to remain strong in our witness when times are hard and our worst fears become realities, as well as when times are easy and we are distracted. Help us escape the lure of drugs, the easy slide into using force to settle our problems, and the snares of our own greed, that we may always speak and act out your love with joy, with compassion for all creatures of your creation, until Christ comes and we feast at the heavenly banquet. Through Jesus, who was given prophetic gifts by travelers from afar and whom Anna and Simeon recognized as the Promised One; with the Holy Spirit, who instructs us in the way of Jesus and awakens the gifts of creativity and vision in your church; all honor and glory are yours, Almighty God, now and into the reaches of eternity. Amen.

The Sovereignty of Jesus

Last Sunday in the season of Pentecost, the fifth Sunday before
December 25
The emphasis of this feast is on Jesus as Sovereign God.

Prayer for the Sovereignty of Jesus

More than a political ruler, the term "sovereignty" connotes royalty. By emphasizing this on the last Sunday before Advent, we are reminded both that Jesus will be born as royalty on December 25 and that the entire church-year cycle of observances has brought us around to seeing Jesus as our ruler in all matters.

O God, we dislike being told what to do. We don't like our behavior to be corrected. We really don't like our rulers and politicians to lord it over us. As adults we are free of our parents' control, and we want to be the only ones to make decisions in our lives. But you are not any ruler. you worry about your people. You treat us as King David regarded his friend Jonathan—with care, respect, and love. Thank you.

Calendar of the Church Year

Most of the major church celebrations are movable festivals; that is, they happen on different dates each year. The few exceptions are Christmas, which is always on December 25, and Epiphany, which is always on January 6. Everything else moves.

Advent, Christmas, and Epiphany

This season runs from the Sunday nearest November 30 (Saint Andrew's Day) to January 6 (Epiphany). Advent can begin anywhere between November 27 and December 2 and comprises the four Sundays preceding December 25. It focuses on preparing for and celebrating the birth of Jesus.

The four to nine Sundays between January 7 and Ash Wednesday are known as the season after Epiphany. This season focuses on Jesus' divinity, ministry, and his training the disciples to share the good news.

Ash Wednesday begins forty-six days before Easter (on the Wednesday before the sixth Sunday before Easter) and signals the start of Lent. This means that Ash Wednesday can fall anywhere between February 6 and March 10. The focus of Lent is on repentance and coming back to God, renewing our baptismal vows.

Easter is celebrated on the first Sunday after the full moon that occurs on or after March 21 (the vernal equinox), provided that if the full moon occurs on a Sunday, Easter is the Sunday afterward. Thus, Easter falls somewhere between March 22 and April 25. The date of Easter determines the length of the season after Epiphany; it also determines the beginning of the seasons of Eastertide and Pentecost. Easter focuses on the rising of Jesus from the dead.

The fifty days from Easter to the day of Pentecost constitute Eastertide. The focus of this season is on celebrating the resurrection of Jesus.

The season of Pentecost extends from the day of Pentecost (May 11–June 13) until the first Sunday in Advent (November 27–December 2). This season focuses on how we live and grow as Christians and on our discipleship and ministry.

Lectionary Years

Each lectionary year begins in Advent.

1999—B

2000—C

2001—A

2002—B

2003—C

2004—A

2005—B

2006—C

2007—A

2008—B

Liturgical, Cultural, and Historical Dates: Day by Day

November

Advent begins on the fourth Sunday before December 25, the Sunday nearest November 30.

27 Earliest date for the start of Advent; Feast Day of Saint James; Feast Day of Saint Paladius; Harvey Milk dies, 1978

28 Berry Gordy Jr. (founder of Motown Records) born, 1929

29 C. S. Lewis born, 1898; Dorothy Day dies, 1980

30 Feast Day of Saint Andrew the apostle; Shirley Chisholm born, 1924; Etty Hillesum dies in Auschwitz, 1943

December

Advent continues, comprising the four Sundays before December 25.

Hanukkah (the Jewish Feast Day of Lights) occurs in November/ December, beginning on the twenty-fifth day of Kislev. In 167 B.C.E., Judas Maccabee led a small group of soldiers against the larger army of the Syrian king Antiochus because the Syrians had defiled the Temple in Jerusalem. The Jews drove the Syrians out of the Temple and rededicated it with holy oil that miraculously lasted eight days. This is the event celebrated during the eight days of Hanukkah.

1 World AIDS Day; Rosa Parks sits in the front of the bus, 1955; Japanese Festival of the Water (Spirit)

2 Latest date for the start of Advent; four churchwomen murdered in El Salvador, 1980

3 Feast Day of Saint Francis Xavier (1506–52)

4 Feast Day of Clement of Alexandria; Rainer Maria Rilke born, 1875; Cesar Chavez jailed twenty days (lettuce boycott)

5 Feast Day of Crispina, African woman martyred at Thebaste in 304 C.E.; Montgomery bus boycott began, 1955

6 Feast Day of Saint Nicholas (died 342 C.E. , in Turkey); Agnes Moorhead born, 1900

7 Feast Day of Saint Ambrose (patron saint of domestic animals, died 397 C.E.); Willa Cather born, 1873

8 Feast Day of Immaculate Conception of Mary; Diego Rivera born, 1886; Martin Luther King Jr. receives the Nobel Peace Prize, 1964

9 John Milton born, 1608; New York City Gay Men's Chorus performs at Carnegie Hall, 1984

10 International Human Rights Day; Thomas Gallaudet born, 1787; Red Cloud (Sioux) dies, 1909

11 Lars Skrefsrud, 1910; Aleksandr Solzhenitsyn born, 1918

12 Feast Day of Our Lady of Guadalupe (Mexico); Joseph Rainey, first African American U.S. congressman sworn into Congress, 1870

13 Saint Lucia's Day (Swedish feast of lights); annual meteor shower

14 Feast Day of John of the Cross (died 1591); Feast Day of Teresa of Avila (died 1582); Drestan, Abbot of Deer (c. 600, Scotland)

15 Feast Day of Saint Eleutherius (Byzantine); Jose Marti born, 1853; Chief Sitting Bull (Hunkpapa Sioux) dies, 1890

16 *Las Posadas* begins; O Sapientia (Scotland); Ludwig van Beethoven born, 1770; Ozone Treaty signed, 1988

17 Feast Day of Saint Ignatius (martyred in Antioch, c. 110 C.E.); the Wright brothers' first flight, 1903

18 Slavery abolished (13th Amendment), 1865; Dorothy Sayers remembered (1893–1957); Operation PUSH founded, 1971

19 Feast Day of Saint Boniface (Byzantine)

20 Sacajawea remembered (Shoshoni guide and peacemaker, 1786–1812)

21 Winter of the hundred slain, 1866; Henrietta Szold born, 1860; Montgomery buses integrated, 1956

22 Winter solstice (Northern Hemisphere); annual meteor shower

23 Juan Ramon Jimenez (Spanish poet) born, 1881; Chico Mendes (Brazil) killed, 1988

24 *Las Posadas* ends; Christmas Eve; John Muir dies, 1914

25 Christmas Day; beginning of the twelve days of Christmas; Quentin Crisp born, 1908

26 Kwanzaa begins; Boxing Day; Feast Day of Saint Stephen the martyr; Jean Toomer born, 1894

27 Second day of Kwanzaa; Feast Day of Saint John (apostle and evangelist)

28 Holy Innocents Day; third day of Kwanzaa; Charles Wesley remembered (1708–1788)

29 Fourth day of Kwanzaa; Feast Day of Saint Thomas Becket; battle of Wounded Knee, 1890; Rainer Maria Rilke dies, 1926

30 Fifth day of Kwanzaa; Feast of the Holy Family; John Howard Yoder dies, 1997

31 Watchnight; sixth day of Kwanzaa; John Wyclif dies (1324–1384)

January

Los Pastores is observed in early January. Martin Luther King Jr. Sunday is observed on the Sunday nearest January 15.

The baptism of Jesus is commemorated on the first Sunday after January 6. The Season after Epiphany begins on January 7 and continues until Ash Wednesday (the earliest date of Ash Wednesday is February 6, the latest is March 10). Chinese New Year occurs between January 10 and February 19. The Jewish holiday of Tu B'shvat, an agricultural holiday that looks forward to the spring planting, is observed on the fifteenth day of Shvat (usually January).

1 Feast of the Circumcision and Naming of Jesus; New Year's Day; World Day of Prayer for Peace; seventh and last day of Kwanzaa; Shogatsu Day of Purification (Japan); Day of the Covenant (Church of South India); Emancipation Proclamation issued, 1865

2 Feast Day of Saints Basil and Gregory of Nazianzus

3 J. R. R. Tolkien born, 1892; Simone Weil born, 1909; first lesbian center in the United States opens (New York City), 1971

4 Annual meteor shower; earth nearest the sun; Louis Braille born, 1809

5 Twelfth Night; Alvin Ailey born, 1931; George Washington Carver dies, 1943

6 Feast of the Epiphany (Christ to the Gentiles); Feast of the Three Magi; Dance Theater of Harlem founded, 1971

7 Zora Neale Hurston born, 1891; DDT banned, 1971

8 Galileo dies, 1642; A. J. Muste born, 1885; Stephen Hawking born, 1942

9 Simone de Beauvoir born, 1908; Joan Baez born, 1941

10 George Washington Carver born, 1886; Robinson Jeffers born, 1887

11 Aldo Leopold (founder of Wilderness Society) born, 1887

12 Southern Christian Leadership Conference founded, 1957; Lorraine Hansberry dies, 1965

13 George Fox dies, 1691; Lawrence Wilder became first African American governor, 1990

14 Harriet Tubman remembered (1821–1913); Albert Schweitzer born, 1875; Chief Joseph (Nez Perce) dies, 1879; Julian Bond born, 1940

15 Martin Luther King Jr. born, 1929

16 Susan Sontag born, 1933

17 Whale migrations along the West Coast; Muhammad Ali born, 1942

18 Week of Christian prayer begins (January 18–25); Feast of the Confession of Saint Peter; A. A. Milne born, 1882

19 John Harold Johnson (publisher of *Ebony*) born, 1918

20 Richard Le Gallienne born, 1866

21 Huddie "Leadbelly" Ledbetter born, 1885

22 August Strindberg born, 1849

23 F. Stendhal born, 1783; 24th Amendment ratified (abolishing the poll tax), 1964

24 Edith Wharton born, 1862; Ernesto Cardenal born, 1925; George Cukor dies, 1985

25 Feast of the Conversion of Saint Paul; Robert Burns born, 1759

26 Republic Day (Church of South India); Eugene Sue born, 1804; Angela Davis born, 1928

27 Wolfgang Amadeus Mozart born, 1756; Lewis Carroll born, 1832

28 Endangered Species Law enacted, 1973

29 Anton Chekhov born, 1860

30 Holiday of the Three Hierarchs (Greek Orthodox); Mohandas Gandhi killed, 1948

31 Jackie Robinson born, 1914; Thomas Merton born, 1915

February

February is designated as Black History Month in the United States. Islamic people also commemorate Mohammed's Ascension during February. Chinese New Year occurs between January 10 and February 19. Hindu people observe Mahashivarathi during February. The Jewish Feast of Purim is celebrated on the thirteenth day of Adar (February to March). It is a remembrance of Queen Esther, who saved the Jewish people from death at the hands of her husband King Ahasuerus of Persia. Purim is a time of celebration and silliness.

Lent usually begins in February. The first day of Lent, Ash Wednesday, occurs on the seventh Wednesday before Easter. (The earliest date is February 6; the latest is March 10.) The Sunday before Ash Wednesday (the last Sunday after Epiphany) is Transfiguration Sunday (although it is observed on August 6 by Catholics and Episcopalians).

1　S. Brigit remembered; Langston Hughes born, 1902; Greensboro Woolworth lunch counter sit-in, 1960

2　Presentation of Jesus in the Temple; Candlemas Day; Groundhog Day

3　Elizabeth Blackwell (first woman doctor) remembered, 1821; Gertrude Stein born, 1874; Simone Weil born, 1909

4　Winter is half over; Rosa Parks born, 1913; Betty Friedan born, 1921; Liberace dies, 1987

5　Henry Aaron born, 1934

6　Earliest date for Ash Wednesday and the beginning of Lent; Bob Marley (Jamaica) born, 1945

7　Eubie Blake born, 1883; Carter Woodson began Negro History Week in 1926

8　Martin Buber born, 1878; Elizabeth Bishop born, 1911

9　Alice Walker born, 1944

10　Boris Pasternak born, 1890; Leontyne Price born, 1927; Bill Sherwood dies, 1990

11　Thomas Edison born, 1847; Nelson Mandela (South Africa) freed, 1990

12　Abraham Lincoln born, 1809; NAACP founded, 1909

13　Georges Simenon born, 1903; S.C.L.C. founded, 1957

14　Feast Day of Saint Valentine (third-century priest in Rome); Frederick Douglass born, 1817

15　Buddha born, 563 B.C.E. ; Susan B. Anthony born, 1820; A. N. Whitehead born, 1862

16　Octave Mirbeau born, 1850

17　Geronimo (Apache) dies, 1909

18　Martin Luther dies, 1546; Toni Morrison born, 1931; Audre Lorde born, 1934

19 Nicolaus Copernicus born, 1473; Japanese American Day of Remembrance (recalling the internment camps) established, 1978

20 Bill Tilden born, 1893; Frederick Douglass dies, 1895; Sidney Poitier born, 1927

21 Peter Damien remembered (1844–1888, Molokai, Hawaii); W. H. Auden born, 1907; Barbara Jordan born, 1936; Campaign for Nuclear Disarmament founded, 1948; Malcolm X assassinated, 1965

22 George Washington born, 1732; Edna St. Vincent Millay born, 1892; Ishmael Reed born, 1938

23 George Frideric Handel born, 1685; W. E. B. DuBois born, 1868; supernova, 1987

24 Wilhelm Grimm born, 1786

25 Anthony Burgess born, 1917

26 Victor Hugo born, 1802

27 Marian Anderson born, 1902; John Steinbeck born, 1902; Christian Haren dies, 1996

28 Michel de Montaigne born, 1533; Phyllis Wheatley (poet) dies, 1784

29 Hattie McDaniel became the first African American to receive an Academy Award, 1940

March

March is designated as Women's History Month in the United States. The third week of March is designated as Central America Week. The Jewish Feast of Purim (Esther) is celebrated on the thirteenth day of Adar (February to March). Passover (Pesac, Feast of Unleavened Bread) is observed on the fourteenth to twenty-first days of Nisan (March to April). Originally a spring festival, it was paired with the Feast of Unleavened Bread to include the symbolism of the tenth plague sent by God upon the Egyptians, the salvation of the firstborn Jewish children, and Jewish liberation from Egyptian slavery.

Lent sometimes begins in March. The first day of Lent, Ash Wednesday, occurs on the seventh Wednesday before Easter. (The earliest date is February 6; the latest is March 10.) The Sunday before Ash Wednesday (the last

Sunday after Epiphany) is Transfiguration Sunday (although it is observed on August 6 by Catholics and Episcopalians). Easter may also occur during March. (The earliest date is March 23; the latest is April 25.) The fifty days of Eastertide begin on Easter Sunday and end on Pentecost Day.

1 George Herbert remembered (1593–1633); Yellowstone National Park founded, 1872; Ralph Ellison born, 1914; Merlie Evers-Williams born, 1933

2 Scholem Aleichem born, 1859; William Stringfellow dies, 1985

3 Doll Festival (Japan); Edmund Waller born, 1606

4 Antonio Vivaldi born, 1678; Jane Goodall born, 1934

5 Isidora (fifth-century "fool for Christ") born; Leontine Kelly (African American bishop) born, 1920

6 Michelangelo born, 1475; Elizabeth Barrett Browning born, 1806; Dred Scott decision 1857; Gabriel Garcia Marquez born, 1928

7 Saint Perpetua and companions martyred (Carthage), 202 C.E.

8 International Women's Day

9 Vita Sackville-West born, 1892; Paula Marshall born, 1929

10 Latest date for Ash Wednesday; Tibet Freedom Day; Angela Saavedra (Spanish poet) remembered, 1791; Harriet Tubman dies, 1913

11 Johnny Appleseed Day; Ralph Abernathy born, 1926

12 Sandhill Crane Watch Day (Nebraska); Jack Kerouac born, 1922; Edward Albee born, 1928

13 Gutenberg Bible published,1462; Kofi Awoonor born, 1935

14 Albert Einstein born, 1879

15 Ides of March; Julius Caesar dies, 44 B.C.E.

16 Arrival of long-billed curlews in Oregon; My Lai Massacre in Vietnam, 1968

17 Saint Patrick's Day; Nat King Cole born, 1919

18 Feast Day of Mechtild of Magdeburg (1209–1282); Andrew Young born, 1932; Unita Blackwell born, 1935

19 Swallows return to Capistrano; Lao Tzu remembered, 550 B.C.E.; Ornette Coleman born, 1930

20 Spring equinox (Northern Hemisphere); Patsy Takemoto Mink (Hawaii) elected to U.S. House of Representatives, 1964

21 J. S. Bach born, 1685; Selma-to-Montgomery march starts, 1965

22 O. E. Rolvaag born, 1876; Marcel Marceau born, 1923; Equal Rights Amendment passed, 1972

23 Earliest date for Easter; World Meteorological Day; Akira Kurosawa born, 1910

24 Archbishop Oscar Romero (El Salvador) killed, 1980; ACT UP's first demonstration, 1987

25 Feast of the Annunciation to Mary; Flannery O'Connor born, 1925; Aretha Franklin born, 1942

26 Robert Frost born, 1874; Anne Frank killed at Bergen-Belsen, 1945

27 Alice Herz born, 1867; Shusaku Endo born, 1923

28 Three Mile Island meltdown, 1979; Mario Vargas Llosa born, 1936

29 Howard Lindsay born, 1889; Pearl Bailey born, 1918

30 Spring Corn Dance (American Indian); Vincent van Gogh born, 1863; African American suffrage, 1870

31 John Donne dies, 1631; Cesar Chavez born, 1927

April

The month of April includes part of Eastertide, which encompasses the fifty days between Easter and Pentecost, beginning March 23 to April 25 and ending May 11 to June 13. The Aztec Spring Festival, the Cherry Blossom Festival, and Spring Planting are celebrated during April. Yom Hashoah, Holocaust Remembrance Day, is observed on the twenty-sixth day of Nisan (March to April).

1 Nazi Germany began persecution of Jews, 1933; Charles Drew (hematologist) dies, 1950

2 James Joyce born, 1882

3 Septima Poinsetta Clark born, 1898; Carter G. Woodson dies, 1950; Martin Luther King Jr.'s "Mountaintop" speech delivered, 1968

4 Maya Angelou born, 1928; Martin Luther King Jr. assassinated (Memphis), 1968

5 Booker T. Washington born, 1856; Colin Powell born, 1937

6 North Pole reached, 1909; Bob Marley born, 1945

7 World Health Day; Billie Holiday born, 1915

8 Benjamin Lindner killed by Contras (Nicaragua), 1986

9 Paul Robeson born, 1898; W. B. Yeats dies, 1939; Dietrich Bonhoeffer killed by Nazis, 1945; Ryan White dies of AIDS at the age of eighteen, 1990; 65,000 March for Equal Rights, 1989

10 Mechtild of Hackenborn remembered; Teilhard de Chardin born, 1881; Frida Kahlo born, 1910; Arthur Ashe born, 1943; Jackie Robinson joins the Dodgers, 1947; first Arbor Day held in Nebraska (date varies by location)

11 Glenway Wescott born, 1901

12 Andrew Young born, 1932

13 Eudora Welty born, 1909

14 Abraham Lincoln killed, 1865; Katherine Dunham (choreographer) born, 1910

15 Titanic sinks, 1912

16 Charlie Chaplin born, 1889; Martin Luther King Jr.'s letter from the Birmingham jail written, 1963

17 Isak Dinesen born, 1885

18 Richard Harding Davis born, 1864

19 Jose Echegaray born, 1832; Dick Sargent born, 1930

20 Chief Pontiac (Ottawa), dies, 1769; Herman Bang born, 1857

21 Annual meteor shower; John Muir born, 1838; Bergen-Belsen liberated, 1945

22 Earth Day instituted, 1970

23 Toyohiko Kagawa (Japan); William Shakespeare born, 1564; UN Law of the Sea passed, 1982

24 World Children's Day; Dorothy Uhnak born, 1930

25 Latest date for Easter; Feast Day of Saint Mark the evangelist (Church of South India); Ella Fitzgerald born, 1918

26 John Audubon born, 1785; Bishop Juan Gerardi (Guatemala) killed, 1998

27 Coretta Scott King born, 1927

28 Tulip Festival (Holland)

29 Saint Catherine of Sienna dies, 1380; Duke Ellington born, 1899; Katherine Forrest born, 1939; American Indian Movement begins, 1968

30 Countee Cullen born, 1903; Annie Dillard born, 1945; Vietnam War ends, 1975

May

May is designated as Asian-Pacific Heritage Month. Mother's Day, which began as a protest against war, is celebrated on the second Sunday of May. Peace Sunday is often celebrated in May, and Memorial Day is observed on the Sunday before May 30.

Ascension Day, often during May, is observed forty days after Easter. Ascension Sunday (May 4–June 6) is the sixth Sunday after Easter. The seventh Sunday after Easter (May 11–June 13) is Pentecost Day. The season of Pentecost begins on Pentecost Day and ends November 26 to December 2. The eighth Sunday after Easter (May 18–June 20) is Trinity Sunday. Shavuot, the Jewish Pentecost (Feast Day of Weeks), is observed fifty days after Passover, in May or June. It began as a celebration of the first fruits of the wheat harvest; later a celebration of the giving of the Torah was added.

1 May Day (the halfway point between spring equinox and summer solstice); Feast Day of Saint Joseph the worker

2 Leonardo da Vinci remembered (1452–1519)

3 Día de la Cruz; Golda Meir born, 1898; U.S. Bishops Peace Pastoral issued, 1983

4 Feast Day of Saint Pelagia of Tarsus (martyr, Eastern Orthodox Church)

5 Cinco de Mayo (Mexico); Søren Kierkegaard born, 1813; Chief Kickingbird (Kiowa) dies, 1875

6 Saint George's Day; Feast Day of John the apostle (Church of South India); Maria Montessori born, 1870

7 Johannes Brahms born, 1833; Rabindranath Tagore born, 1862

8 Julian of Norwich remembered (1342–after 1416); Peter Maurin born, 1876; Gary Snyder born, 1930

9 Daniel Berrigan born, 1921

10 NAACP incorporated, 1910; Judith Jamison born, 1943

11 Earliest date for Day of Pentecost

12 Florence Nightingale born, 1820; H. Rap Brown becomes chair of the S.N.C.C., 1967

13 Stevie Wonder born, 1950

14 Mochuda of Lismore remembered (Irish Church), 637 C.E..

15 Feast Day of Saints Isidore and Maria (patron saints of farm workers); International Conscientious Objectors' Day

16 Victoria Day (Canada); Native American Day; Joan of Arc born, 1412

17 Syttende Mai (holiday); Supreme Court desegregation ruling, 1954

18 Earliest date for Trinity Sunday; Mary McLeod Bethune dies, 1955

19 Malcolm X born, 1925

20 Bread for the World instituted, 1974

21 Lag B'omer (holiday); Fats Waller born, 1904; Raymond Burr born, 1917

22 Benjamin Davis Jr. becomes first African American general in U.S. Air Force, 1959; Langston Hughes dies, 1967; Harvey Milk born, 1930

23 Cherokee Nation forced to vacate all land east of the Mississippi River (the "Trail of Tears"), 1839

24 Feast Day of Saints Cyril and Methodius (missionaries to Czechoslovakia); Duke Ellington dies, 1974

25 Miles Davis born, 1926

26 Charles Anderson (Kentucky) born, 1907

27 Rachel Carson (environmentalist) born, 1903

28 Sierra Club founded, 1892

29 U.S. Navy concludes that homosexuals in the military do not create a security risk, 1957

30 Memorial Day (U.S.) began when Southern women honored the graves of both sides after the Civil War battle of Shiloh

31 Walt Whitman remembered (1819–1892); G. K. Chesterton born, 1874; Gloria Molina born, 1948

June

June is designated as Lesbian and Gay History Month, and the last Sunday of the month is Gay/Lesbian Pride Sunday. The third Sunday in June is Father's Day.

Ascension Day, sometimes during June, is observed forty days after Easter. Ascension Sunday (May 4–June 6) is the sixth Sunday after Easter. The seventh Sunday after Easter (May 11–June 13) is Pentecost Day. The season of Pentecost begins on Pentecost Day and ends November 26 to December 2. The eighth Sunday after Easter (May 18–June 20) is Trinity Sunday. Shavuot, the Jewish Pentecost (Feast Day of Weeks), is observed fifty days after Passover, in May or June.

1 Slavery begins in Virginia, 1619; Harriet Tubman born, 1826; Father Jacques Marquette born, 1637

2 Rice Harvest Festival (Japan); Native American citizenship, 1924

3 Feast Day of Lucillian and companions (martyrs, Eastern Orthodox Church); Pope John XXIII dies, 1963

4 International Day of Innocent Children, victims of aggression

5 World Environmental Day (instituted 1972); James Meredith's "March against Fear," 1966

6 Marian Edelman born, 1939; Robert Kennedy killed, 1968

7 Chief Seattle (Suquamish) dies, 1866; Gwendolyn Brooks born, 1917; Nikki Giovanni born, 1943

8 Mohammed dies, 632 C.E. ; Aedh of Terryglass (Ireland) dies, 842 C.E.

9 Columba of Iona dies, 597 C.E.

10 Feast Day of the Sacred Heart of Jesus; founding of Alcoholics Anonymous, 1935

11 Feast Day of Barnabas the Apostle (Church of South India); G. M. Hopkins born, 1844

12 Djuna Barnes born, 1892; Barbara Harris (Episcopal bishop) born, 1930; Medgar Evers dies, 1963

13 Latest date for Pentecost Day; Thurgood Marshall appointed to U.S. Supreme Court, 1967

14 William Gray (African American) elected House Democratic Whip, 1989

15 Magna Carta, 1215

16 Soweto (South Africa) Massacre, 1976; Spelman College opens, 1881

17 Linda Chavez born, 1947; Stokely Carmichael calls for the Black Power movement, 1966

18 Unita Blackwell (first woman African American mayor in Mississippi) born, 1933

19 King James I (England, authorized the K.J.V. Bible) born, 1566; Juneteenth, slaves in Texas find out about the Emancipation Proclamation signed on January 1 (Black Emancipation Day), 1865

20 Latest date for Trinity Sunday; Midsummer's Eve

21 Summer begins (Northern Hemisphere; first full day)

22 Joe Lewis becomes the heavyweight boxing champion, 1937

23 Willie Mae Ford (gospel singer) born, 1904; Wilma Rudolph born, 1940

24 Feast Day of John the Baptist (Church of South India); Henry Ward Beecher born, 1813

25 Native American Day; battle of Little Big Horn, 1876

26 National University of El Salvador attacked by the army (26 killed), 1980

27 Emma Goldman born, 1869; Paul Dunbar (poet) born, 1872; Helen Keller born, 1880

28 Gay/Lesbian Pride Day; John Wesley remembered (1703–1791); Stonewall rebellion, 1969

29 Feast Day of Peter the apostle (Church of South India); Anne Frank born, 1929

30 Czeslaw Milosz born, 1911

July

1 Canada Day; John Bunyan born, 1629; Charles Laughton born, 1899; Benjamin Davis Sr. (first African American Army general) born, 1877

2 Thomas Cranmer remembered (1489–1556); Aldo Leopold born, 1907; Thurgood Marshall born, 1908; Medgar Evers born, 1925; Civil Rights Act passed, 1964

3 Chief Little Crow (Sioux) dies, 1863; Jackie Robinson inducted into the baseball Hall of Fame, 1962

4 U.S. Independence Day

5 Earth farthest from the sun

6 Jan Hus born, 1369, dies, 1415; Pablo Neruda born, 1904

7 Satchel Paige born, 1904

8 Dorothy Thompson (journalist) born, 1894; Alice Faye Wattleton born, 1943

9 June Jordan born, 1936

10 John Calvin remembered (1509–1564); Marcel Proust born, 1871

11 World Population Day

12 Henry David Thoreau born, 1817; Bill Cosby born, 1937

13 Synaxis of the archangel Gabriel (Eastern Orthodox Church)

14 Kateri Tekakwitha (Mohawk) born, 1656; Bastille Day, 1880; Isaac Bashevis Singer born, 1904

15 Feast Day of Saint Swithun of Winchester (Scottish Church, 862 C.E.); Rembrandt born, 1606

16 Feast Day of Scotha of Clonmore (Ireland); Katherine Ortega born, 1934; first A-Bomb detonated, 1945

17 Port Chicago ammunition explosion kills over two hundred African Americans, 1944

18 Nelson Mandela born, 1918

19 Feast Day of Saint Vincent de Paul; First women's rights conference, 1848; Temple Beth Chayim Chadashim becomes first U.S. Gay and Lesbian synagogue, 1974; Mark Wellman begins climbing El Capitan in Yosemite, 1989

20 Geneva Convention (peace agreement on Korea and Indochina), 1954

21 Feast Day of Saint Simeon (Eastern Orthodox Church)

22 Feast Day of Mary Magdalene (Church of South India); Gregor Mendel born, 1822

23 Fourteenth Amendment ratified, granting citizenship to all African Americans, 1868

24 Simon Bolivar remembered (1783–1830); Signing of Peace Treaty by Chief Pontiac, 1766

25 Feast Day of James the Apostle (Church of South India)

26 Carl Jung born, 1875; Americans with Disabilities Act signed into law, 1990

27 Annual meteor shower (through July 29)

28 Johann Sebastian Bach dies, 1750; Judy Grahn born, 1940

29 Dag Hammarskjöld born, 1905

30 James Varick becomes the first bishop of the African Methodist Episcopal Zion Church, 1822

31 Feast Day of Saint Ignatius Loyola; Bartholome de las Casas dies, 1506; Whitney Young Jr. born, 1921

August

World Peace Day is observed on the First Sunday in August. In early August, American Indians hold intertribal celebrations.

1 Lammas Day (the midway point between summer solstice and autumn equinox)

2 James Baldwin born, 1924

3 Flannery O'Connor dies, 1964; Georgia police arrest Michael Hardwick for sodomy, 1982

4 The bodies of three civil rights workers are found outside Philadelphia, Mississippi, 1964

5 James Cone (theologian) born, 1938; Vitto Russo (journalist) dies, 1990

6 Feast of the Transfiguration of Christ (Catholic, Episcopal, and Church of South India); Hiroshima bombing, 1945; Voting Rights Act signed, 1965; Minnesota removes transgender discrimination, 1993

7 Ralph Bunche born, 1904; first photo of earth from Explorer VI, 1969

8 Executive order requiring equal employment opportunities in all federal agencies, 1969

9 F. Jaegerstetter dies, 1943; Nagasaki bombing,1945; Adoniram Judson born, 1788

10 Saint Laurence dies, 258 C.E. (martyr, Scottish Church)

11 Clare of Assisi dies, 1253; John Rosamond Johnson (composer of the black national anthem, "Lift Every Voice and Sing") born, 1873

12 Annual meteor shower; Radclyffe Hall born, 1880

13 Feast Day of Saint Maximus, confessor (Eastern Orthodox Church)

14 S. Max Kolbe dies at Auschwitz; Social Security Act ratified, 1935

15 Feast Day of the Assumption of Mary; Independence Day (Church of South India); Oscar Romero born, 1917

16 Wyatt Tee Walker (S.C.L.S. director) born, 1929

17 Marcus Garvey born, 1887

18 Confucius born, 551 B.C. ; James Meredith graduates from the University of Mississippi, 1963

19 Ralph Bunche named undersecretary of the United Nations, 1954

20 Fallen Timbers Massacre, 1794; Paul Tillich born, 1886; Bernard of Clairvaux born (1090–1153)

21 Sionach of Clonard dies, 588 C.E. (Irish Church); Count Basie born, 1904

22 Nat Turner begins a slave revolt in Virginia, 1831

23 Feast Day of Saints Luppus and Irenaeus (martyrs, Eastern Orthodox Church); Nina Simone born, 1933

24 Jorge Luis Borges born, 1899; Marlee Matlin born, 1965

25 Leonard Bernstein born, 1925; Althea Gibson born, 1927

26 19th Amendment (women's suffrage), 1920 (Women's Equality Day)

27 Mother Teresa born, 1910; W. E. B. DuBois dies, 1963

28 Elizabeth Seton born, 1774; Leo Tolstoy, born, 1828; Martin Luther King's "I Have a Dream" speech (Washington D.C.), 1963; first Gay Games (San Francisco), 1982

29 Beheading of John the Baptist; Simone Weil dies, 1943

30 Fiachra of Breuil dies, 650 C.E. (Irish Church)

31 Feast Day of Aidan of Lindisfarne; Cherokee national holidays

September

The period from September 15 to October 15 is designated as Hispanic Heritage Month. The first Monday in September is Labor Day. Churches also observe Homecoming Sunday and Christian Education Sunday during September.

Several Jewish holidays occur during the month of Tishri (September to October). Rosh Hashanah (New Year) is the first day of Tishri. Yom Kippur (Day of Atonement) is on the tenth; it is observed by fasting and mourning, admitting mistakes, and asking forgiveness. In ancient times, the observance was concluded by transferring the people's sins onto a scapegoat, which was released in the desert. Sukkoth (Feast of the Tabernacles), is observed on the fifteenth to twenty-second days of Tishri. Initially it was a ceremony of gratitude toward God that concluded the gathering of the crops. Over time, the meaning of the tents put up for the celebration came to include gratitude to God for the exodus which led them out of slavery and into freedom in the desert. Simchat Torah is observed on the twenty-third day of Tishri. It marks when one year's reading of the Torah ends and a new one begins.

 1 Greek New Year's Day

 2 Feast Day of John the Faster (sixth-century patriarch of Constantinople, Eastern Orthodox Church)

 3 Loren Eiseley born, 1907

 4 Richard Wright born, 1908

 5 Chief Crazy Horse (Oglala) dies, 1877

 6 Hiroshigi remembered (1797–1858); Jane Addams born, 1860

 7 United Tribes Days begin; Grandma Moses born, 1860

 8 International Literacy Day

 9 Chrysanthemum Festival (Japan)

10 Feast Day of Finian of Moville (scholar, early Irish Church)

11 Feast Day of Theodora of Alexandria (Eastern Orthodox Church)

12 Irène Joliot-Curie born, 1897; Jesse Owens born, 1913; *The Advocate* begins publication, 1967; Steven Biko dies, 1977

13 Dante Alighieri dies, 1321

14 Holy Cross Day (Triumph of the Cross)

15 Claude McKay born, 1889; Anne Moody born, 1940; Birmingham bombing, 1963

16 Hidalgo's Cry for Freedom, 1810; Mexican Independence Day, 1821; B. B. King born, 1925

17 Feast Day of Hildegard of Bingen

18 Congress passes the Fugitive Slave Act, 1850

19 Feast Day of Theodore of Tarsus (Scottish Church)

20 Feast Day of Saints Michael and Theodora (martyrs, Eastern Orthodox Church)

21 International Day of Peace; Feast Day of Matthew the apostle (Church of South India)

22 Autumn equinox (Northern Hemisphere); Ralph Bunche born, 1904; Peace Corps founded, 1961

23 Feast Day of Adamnan, Abbot of Iona (Scottish Church); John Coltrane born, 1926

24 Native American Day

25 Little Rock (Arkansas) Central High School integrated by force, 1957

26 Johnny Appleseed born, 1774; T. S. Eliot born, 1888

27 Inauguration of the union of the Church of South India

28 Diarmaid of Feenagh (County Leitrim, Irish Church)

29 Feast Day of Saint Michael and all the angels (Michael, Gabriel and Raphael); Leif Ericson Day

30 Saint Jerome's Day; Elie Wiesel born, 1928

October

October is designated as Domestic Violence Awareness Month in the United States. Many Christian churches celebrate the first Sunday in October as Worldwide Communion Sunday and the Sunday before October 31 as Reformation Sunday.

The Jewish holiday of Sukkoth (Feast Day of Tabernacles) is observed on the fifteenth to twenty-second days of Tishri (September to October), to celebrate the end of the agricultural season. Simchat Torah (the beginning of a new year of reading) is observed on the twenty-third day of Tishri. The Hindu festival of lights, Diwali, is celebrated for three nights in October to November to mark the end of the monsoon season.

1 Mohammed's birth; Yosemite National Park founded, 1890; World Habitat Day

2 Mohandas Gandhi born, 1869; Guardian Angels founded

3 Frank Robinson becomes major league baseball's first African American manager, 1974

4 Saint Francis of Assisi dies, 1226; H. Rap Brown born, 1943

5 Feast Day of Saint Charitina (martyr, Eastern Orthodox Church); Tecumseh (Shawnee) dies, 1813

6 Feast Day of Thomas the apostle (Church of South India); William Tyndale dies, 1536; Fannie Lou Hamer born, 1917

 7 Desmond Tutu born, 1931; Leroi Jones born, 1934; Toni Morrison wins the Nobel Prize for Literature, 1993

 8 Great Chicago fire, 1871; Jesse Jackson born, 1941

 9 Feast Day of Denys of Paris (Scottish Church); Leif Erickson Day

10 Canadian Thanksgiving; Eleanor Roosevelt born, 1884; Thelonious Monk born, 1917

11 Feast Day of Saint Philip (Eastern Orthodox Church); Cleve Jones (Names AIDS Memorial Quilt founder) born, 1954

12 Indigenous Peoples Day; Columbus Day; Dick Gregory born, 1932

13 Congan, dies, 735 C.E. (Scottish Church)

14 W. Penn dies, 1718; first gay and lesbian civil rights march on Washington, D.C., 1979

15 Feast Day of Saint Teresa of Avila (1515–1582); Nelson Mandela and F. W. de Klerk named co-winners of Nobel Peace Prize, 1993

16 World Food Day; Día de la Raza; Million Man March, 1995

17 Black Poetry Day

18 Feast Day of Saint Luke (Church of South India); Ntozake Shange born, 1948; Wynton Marsalis born, 1961

19 James Meredith escorted into University of Mississippi, 1962

20 Feast Day of Saint Artemius (Eastern Orthodox Church); Christopher Wren remembered (1632–1723)

21 Feast Day of the Black Christ

22 250,000 people boycott in Chicago over school segregation, 1963

23 Swallows leave Capistrano

24 World Disarmament Day; UN Charter signed, 1945

25 Saint Crispin's Day; Northern Ireland repeals its sodomy laws, 1982

26 Feast Day of Kela (female saint, early Irish Church)

27 Feast Day of Nestor, companion of Demetrius (Eastern Orthodox Church); Ruby Dee born, 1927

28 National Immigrants Day; Desiderius Erasmus dies, 1536

29 Feast Day of Taimhthionna (early female saint of Ireland)

30 Racial segregation in the U.S. armed forces ends, 1954

31 All Hallows' Eve; Halloween; Luther nails the ninety-five theses

November

November is designated as Native American Heritage Month in the United States. Thanksgiving Day is celebrated on the fourth Thursday of November, and the Sunday before Thanksgiving Day is Thanksgiving Sunday.

Advent begins on the fourth Sunday before December 25, the Sunday nearest November 30. The Sunday before the beginning of Advent commemorates the Sovereignty of Christ.

For three nights in October or November, Diwali, the Hindu festival of lights, celebrates the end of the monsoon season.

 1 All Saints' Day (lesser saints)

 2 All Souls' Day (the departed); Day of the Dead (Mexico); Carol Moseley Braun elected to the U.S. Senate, 1992

 3 Feast Day of Martin de Porres (patron saint of social justice)

 4 Feast Day of Joannicius the Great (Eastern Orthodox Church); Essex Hemphill (poet) dies, 1995

 5 World Community Day

 6 Derrick Bell (African American professor at Harvard) born, 1930

 7 Fionntan of Strasbourg dies, 687 C.E. (Irish Church)

 8 Dorothy Day born, 1897

 9 Dorothy Dandridge born, 1923; Kristallnacht (beginning of the Holocaust), 1938

10 Martin Luther born, 1483

11 Veterans Day; Fyodor Dostoevsky born, 1821; Martin Luther King Sr. dies, 1984

12 Feast Day of Machar (c. 600, Scottish Church)

13 Feast Day of John Chrysostom (Eastern Orthodox Church); Whoopi Goldberg born, 1955; Karen Silkwood dies, 1975

14 Booker T. Washington dies, 1915

15 Feast Day of Saint Fergus (Scottish Church)

16 Martyrs of the Jesuit University die (San Salvador), 1989

17 Feast Day of Aengus of Strangford Lough (Irish Church)

18 Hilda dies, 680 (Scottish Church); Howard Thurman born, 1900; Dr. Evelyn Hooker (documented the psychological normality of homosexuality) dies, 1996

19 Feast Day of Abdias (prophet, Eastern Orthodox Church); , Sojourner Truth born, 1797; Abraham Lincoln delivers the Gettysburg Address, 1863

20 Edmund of East Anglia dies, 870 (Scottish Church); Pauli Murray (first African American female priest in the Episcopal Church) born, 1910

21 Feast Day of the Cosmic Christ, Christ the Omega

22 Harry Edwards (sociologist) born, 1942

23 Feast Day of Saint Roinne (Irish Church); U.S. Supreme Court rules in favor of reverse discrimination, 1989

24 Junipero Serra born, 1713; Ron Dellums born, 1935

25 Feast Day of Catherine of Alexandria; John XXIII born, 1881; the ICC bans segregation on all buses, 1955

26 Sojourner Truth dies (American visionary, preacher, abolitionist, 1797–1883)

Dates of Significance for Ethnic/Cultural Groups

These dates are drawn from the preceding calendar to suggest observances that may be especially meaningful for people of various ethnic and cultural identities. These lists are not meant to be exhaustive. Individuals or committees within the congregation may make valuable additions.

African American

January 15	Martin Luther King Jr. born, 1929
February	Black History Month
March 21	Selma-to-Montgomery march begins, 1965
April 3	Martin Luther King Jr.'s "Mountaintop" speech, 1968
May 19	Malcolm X born, 1925
June 19	Juneteenth, 1865
July 9	June Jordan born, 1936
August 11	John Rosamond Johnson born, 1873
September 15	Four girls killed in Birmingham bombing, 1963
October 7	Toni Morrison wins Nobel Prize for Literature, 1993
November 18	Howard Thurman born, 1900
December 1	Rosa Parks sits in the front of the bus and the Montgomery Bus Boycott soon begins, 1955
December 26	Kwanzaa begins (through January 1)

Asian American

January 10–February 19	Chinese New Year
Febuary 19	Japanese American Day of Remembrance (recalling World War II internment camps)
March 20	Patsy Takemoto Mink, first Asian American woman elected to the U.S. House of Representatives, 1964
April	Cherry Blossom Festival
May	Asian-Pacific Heritage Month
June 2	Rice Harvest Festival (Japan)
July 22	Feast Day of Mary Magdalene (South India)
August 6	Hiroshima Day
September 9	Chrysanthemum Festival (Japan)

October 18   Feast Day of Saint Luke (South India)

November   Diwali, Festival of Lights (India)

December 6   Feast Day of Saint Nicholas (Turkey)

Persons with Disabilities

January 4   Louis Braille (teacher, blind) born, 1809

January 8   Stephen Hawking (physicist, ALS) born, 1942

Febuary 11   Thomas Edison born, 1847

June   John Hockenberry (journalist, paraplegic) born, 1956

June 27   Helen Keller (lecturer, blind and deaf) born, 1880

July 19   Mark Wellman (paraplegic) begins climbing El Capitan in Yosemite, 1989

July 26   Americans with Disabilities Act passed, 1990

August 24   Marlee Matlin (actor, deaf) born, 1965

November 13   Whoopi Goldberg (actor, dyslexia) born, 1955

December 10   Thomas Gallaudet (educator of the deaf) born, 1787

December 16   Ludwig van Beethoven (composer, became deaf) born, 1770

European American

January 14   Albert Schweitzer born, 1875

February 21   Peter Damien

March 6   Elizabeth Barrett Browning born, 1806

April 29   Catherine of Sienna dies, 1380

May 16   Joan of Arc born, 1412

June 9   Columba of Iona dies, 597

July 6   Jan Hus born, 1369

August 9   F. Jaegerstetter dies, 1943

September 12   Irène Joliot-Curie born, 1897

October 4   Francis of Assisi dies, 1226

November 8   Dorothy Day born, 1897

December 11 Lars Skrefsrud born, 1910

December 18 Dorothy Sayers born, 1893

Gay/Lesbian

January 3   First lesbian center in the United States (New York City), 1971

Febuary 3   Gertrude Stein born, 1874

Febuary 8   Elizabeth Bishop born, 1911

March 24   ACT UP's first demonstration, 1987

April 30   Countee Cullen born, 1903

May 22   Harvey Milk born, 1930

June   Lesbian and Gay History Month

July 28   Judy Grahn born, 1940

August 6   Minnesota removes transgender discrimination, 1993

September 12 *The Advocate* begins publication, 1967

October 14   First gay/lesbian civil rights march on Washington, D.C., 1979

November 4   Essex Hemphill (poet) dies, 1995

December 1   World AIDS Day

December 7   Willa Cather born, 1873

Hispanic American

Early January *Los Pastores*

March 24   Oscar Romero killed, 1980

March 31   Cesar Chavez born, 1927

April10   Frida Kahlo (painter) born, 1910

May 5   Cinco de Mayo

June 17   Linda Chavez born, 1947

July 16   Katherine Ortega born, 1934

August 24   Jorge Luis Borges born, 1899

September 15 Hispanic Heritage Month (through October 15)

September 16 Mexican Independence Day, 1821

November 24 Junipero Serra born, 1713

December 12 Feast Day of Our Lady of Guadalupe (Mexico)

December 16 *Las Posadas* (through December 24)

Jewish American

January 3   Simone Weil born, 1909

Febuary 8   Martin Buber born, 1878

March 2   Scholem Aleichem born, 1859

April 21   Liberation of Bergen-Belsen, 1945

May 3   Golda Meir born, 1898

June 29   Anne Frank born, 1929

July 14   Isaac Bashevis Singer born, 1904

August 25   Leonard Bernstein born, 1925

September 30 Elie Wiesel born, 1928

October   Sukkoth (Feast Day of Tabernacles)

November 9   Kristallnacht, 1938

December 21   Henrietta Szold born, 1860

American Indian

Weekly Pow-wows held throughout the year

January 14   Chief Joseph (Nez Perce) dies, 1879

Febuary 17   Geronimo (Apache) dies, 1909

March 30   Spring Corn Dance

April 29   American Indian Movement begins, 1968

May 23	Cherokee Nation forced west, 1839
June 2	Native American citizenship, 1924
July 14	Kateri Tekakwitha (Mohawk) born, 1656
Early August	Intertribal celebrations begin
September 5	Chief Crazy Horse (Oglala) dies, 1877
October 12	Indigenous Peoples Day
November	Native American Heritage Month
December 20	Sacajawea (Shoshoni guide and peacemaker)

Women

January 9	Simone de Beauvoir born, 1908
Febuary 15	Susan B. Anthony born, 1820
March	Women's History Month
March 5	Leontine Kelly (Methodist bishop) born, 1920
April 10	Mechtild of Hackenborn
May 8	Julian of Norwich (1342–after 1416)
June 12	Barbara Harris (Episcopal bishop) born, 1930
July 19	First women's rights conference, 1848
August 26	19th Amendment (women's suffrage), 1920
September 6	Jane Addams born, 1860
October 26	Feast Day of Kela (early female saint, Ireland)
November 2	Carol Moseley Braun, first African American woman elected to the U.S. Senate, 1992
December 2	Four churchwomen killed in El Salvador, 1980

Index of Worship Resources

Liturgics: Calls to Worship, Litanies, Responsive Readings, Services

Hymns, Meditations, Poems, Readings, Stories

Hymns

Meditations

Poems

Readings

Stories

Prayers

Scriptures